INDEX

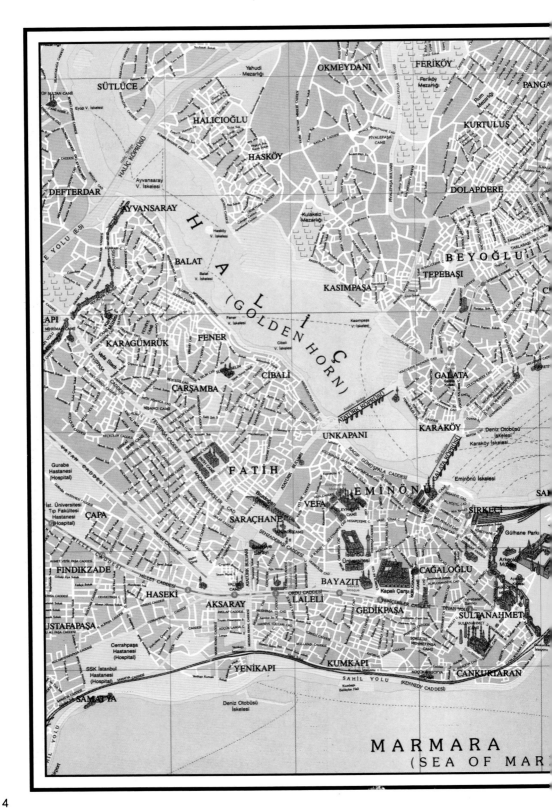

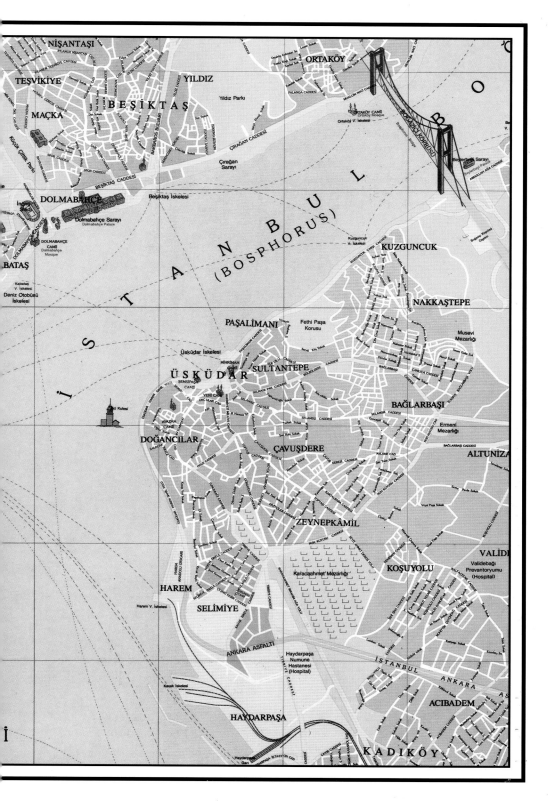

5

THE CITY OF ISTANBUL

Istanbul is the largest city in the Republic of Turkey. It is situated on the shores of the Bosphorus, and is bordered to the north by the Black Sea, to the east by the region of Kocaeli and the Marmara Sea and to the west by Tekirdağ and the Kırklareli region. The city covers a total area of 5712km^2 including, within the urban district, the islands of the Marmara known as the Princes Islands. It is flanked by a high range of hills to the east of the Bosphorus, the highest of which is Aydos (573 m.) near Kartal. Çamlica hill (229 m.) east of Üsküdar, is a recognised tourist spot. Forests surround the city sporadically, the most extensive being the Belgrad Forest which is 20 kms. to the north of the city.

Istanbul winters are warm and wet, summers hot and dry. The climate is tempered by warm Mediterranean winds which counter frequent Black Sea cold fronts. Temperatures vary moderately between day and night, and from season to season. The summer season is approximately 90 days long, while winter is 80 days long. Snow falls for an average of 7 days in a year.

The largest river in the region is the Riva, which flows into the Black Sea. In addition there are two rivers flowing into the Bosphorus, Istinye Deresi and Büyük Dere. The region also boasts three small but notable lakes, all on the European shores of the Bosphorus. These are the fresh-water Terkos, which supplies the cit-

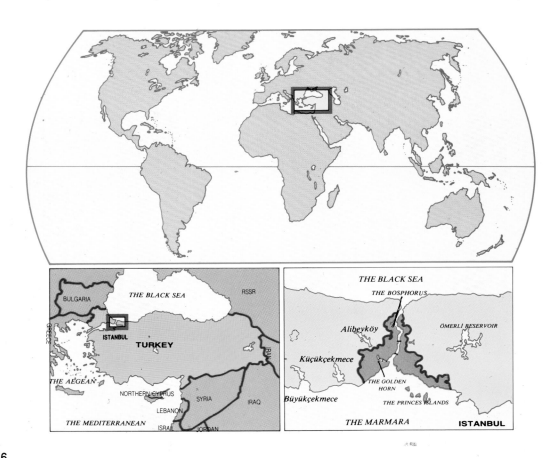

y with much of its water, and the inland seas of Küçük Çekmece and Büyük Çekmece on the Marmara coast, which are salt water lagoons. Fish are found in both these lakes, which are situated in game areas.

The city, whose population is 9.5 million, is a major port and trade centre. It is the most important city in Turkey, possessing a number of universities, high schools, libraries and cultural centres. The city is an impressive sight, situated, as it is, on a site dominating both the Golden Horn and the Bosphorus, and brimming with fine monuments and artefacts of the Byzantine and Ottoman era.

Up to the Turkish conquest of Istanbul by Mehmet II in 1453, the city was the centre of the Byzantine empire. After that date it became the centre of the Ottoman empire. After the founding of the Turkish Republic in 1923, the capital of Turkey became Ankara.

Drawing of the conquest of Constantinople by Mehmet the Conqueror

Aerial view of the Seraglio Point, showing Topkapı Palace, Hagia Sofia and Sultanahmet

EARLY SETTLEMENT AND GROWTH

Although it is not known exactly when the nucleus of the ancient city of Byzantion was founded there is a legend relating to the early settlement of Istanbul. According to the legend, Byzas and his followers of Megara, near Athens, consulted the oracle of Delphi about building a new city, and were advised to build their city "opposite the land of the blind". On hearing this, the men of Megara left their country and travelled the long journey to Istanbul's Seraglio Point (Sarayburnu). Looking across from this vantage point they saw the Phoenician colony of Chalcedon (Kadiköy). Astonished at the blindness of the colonists who had failed to see the beauty of the Seraglio Point, they proclaimed Chalcedon the oracle's "city of the blind", founding their city between the Golden Horn and the point of Lygos. They named it Byzantion, after their leader. Some time later, colonists from Argos also settled there, and before long Byzantion grew from a small town into an important merchantile centre, due to its strategic geographical position. The city was colonised by the Greeks during the Hellenistic invasion in 750-550 B.C., although its geographical position would suggest that there had been previous colonisation on the site. Traces of settlement dating from the end of the fourth millenium to the beginning of the third millenium have been found at Fikirtepe, in Kadiköy. Archeological evidence of settlement in the 7 century B.C. was also found in the IInd court of Topkapı Palace, in 1937, in the form of Proto-Corinthian

Sarayburnu (Seraglio Point) and the entry to the Bosphorus, engraving

sherds.

We may say that the city of Byzantion began to take form during the period of Greek colonisation towards 660 B.C. Its first important historical role was during the Persian invasions of 479 B.C. when the city was won back from the Persians by Pausanias, king of Sparta, at the battle of Platae. Later, the city maintained its independence in the struggle between Athens and Sparta for supremacy by being allied with the more powerful of the protagonists. From time to time the city became extremely important, although occasionally losing its importance altogether.

The earliest city of Byzantion was surrounded by a wall with 27 towers. It was in the district of the present Sarayburnu, and from a topographical point of view, it was similarly placed to many cities of the same are. The walls, which stretched from Sirkeci to Ahırkapı, have left no visible trace at the present ground level. Believed to have been the most sturdy defence system of their time, the walls were of ashlar. A second wall separated the city proper from the Acropolis. The walls were believed to have been built under the guidance of Apollo and Poseidon, with a special constructional technique which provided them with amazing accoustics enabling those within to hear everything that was said on the exterior.

After the city had been besieged by Philip of Macedonia in 340 B.C., the walls were restored with tombstones, hence their title of Tymbosyne.

Two or three harbours were situated at Sirkeci, where the sea and land walls joined. The most important of these was Neorion (Eminönü), to the east of which was the port of Bosphorion or Pro-

Bosphorus Villa, engraving

sphorion. Flanked by stone quays, these harbours were protected by towers at the mouth across which were stretched chains.

The Acropolis, the most sacred area of the city, was situated somewhere near the site of the present Ayasofya (the Byzantine cathedral of St. Sophia), and was reached via steps. Nearby was an agora surrounded by columned arcades and a statue of Helios in the centre. The arcaded agora was known as the Tetrastoon. The city's water was stored in large cisterns. The largest baths in the city were the Akylleos Baths, which stood beside the Thracian Gate (Thrakion Pili). It is known that temples were built in honour of the gods and goddesses Athena, Poseidon and Zeis on the Seraglio Point, while there are traces of a shrine to Hecata in the district of Sultanahmed, and others to Aphrodite, Artemis and Dionysos in and around Topkapi palace. The necropolis was outside the main walls, and stretched from Çemberlitaş to Bayezit. Several excavations in the area yielded tombstones and mausoleums.

During the period of the Roman empire, Byzantion took the side of Pescenius Niger (193-194) against Septimus Severus (192-211), by shutting off the road to Asia. Although Niger was defeated and killed in 194 A.D., the city continued to resist the attacks of Septimus Severus. After a two-year siege, the citizens of Byzantion, having had to resort to cannibalism in their desperation, finally surrendered. The city was severely punished, stripped of its city title and the walls demolished, while soldiers and bureaucrats were put to the sword. It was a calamity for the city which later turned to its advantage. Septimus Severus soon realised the necessity of developing the

The Hippodrome, Sultanahmet mosque and obelisques in engraving

city. He restored the walls and built many new buildings, restoring Byzantion to its city status. In 203 A.D. he began building a hippodrome which, however, remained unfinished on his leaving the city and subsequent death. It is known that the emperor built the Zeuksippos baths between the Hagia Sofia and the hippodrome, a theatre on Seraglio Point, near the temple of Aphrodite and a stadium on the northern slope. He also restored several temples, namely the temples of Zeus, Aphrodite, Apollo, Artemis, Poseidon and Demeter, repaired the harbours and constructed a grand columned 'via' through the city. The road was on the site of the modern Divan Yolu and stretched from the Hippodrome to the main gate in the land walls.

Severus also constructed the huge Caminia baths, which held 2000 people. The site of the baths is not certain, although they were thought to have been outside the walls. As the city grew, the Necropolis began to extend beyond Beyazit.

During the IV century, Byzantion again became the stage of conflict during the power struggle between Constaninus Magnus (Constantine) (306-337 A.D.) and his political opponents. One of these, Licinius I (307-323 A.D.) captured Byzantion, but the city was later restored to the rule of Constantine.

The later Roman emperors felt the need to break away from Rome. Byzantion was an ideal choice as a new capital. Although close to potential enemies to the north and east, it was well fortified and easily defended, and therefore ideal from a military point of view. It was economically ideal being situated on the major trade routes between Asia and Europe, and politically attractive due to its distance

The Bosphorus, engraving

from the intrigues and unrest of the old empire.

Constantine planned to rebuild the city and declare it the second Roman capital. Work on the construction of a new city was begun in 325 A.D., by removing the walls further west. The new city was declared open on 11 May, 330 A.D. with great pomp and ceremony, although the construction of many buildings was to take several more years. The city was called Roma Nova or Roma Secunda - the new or second Rome, and possessed all the priviledges of ancient Rome. Many leading Roman families were brought to settle to aid the city's development. At first the city was ruled by a Proconsul and later by a Praefectus. By moving the walls 2 - 2.5 kms. west, Constantine enlarged the city immediately. As in Rome, it was divided into 14 administrative Regiones, 12 of which were within the walls. Among those outside the walls was Galata, while the furthest district was the Blachernai, now between Edirnekapi and Ayvansaray.

The titles and functions of all the buildings in these regions were recorded in a document dating to the V century, from which we learn of the existance of large numbers of private palaces. At the centre of the columned way running through the city, the road opened out into an oval piazza, the Forum Constantini, in the centre of which stood the porphyry monument which today stands at Çemberlitaş.

The Grand Palace of the emperor was constructed between the Hippodrome and the Sea of Marmara, near the present Sultanahmet mosque. The hippodrome was completed and adorned with a number of monuments and statuary, two temples being built near the Hagia Sophia devoted to Rhea and Tyche. The first Hagia Sophia and Havarion churches were also built dur-

The Süleymaniye Mosque and the Golden Horn (XIX. cent.)

ing this period.

The task of aggrandizing the city was carried on during the reign of Julian (355-363 A.D.). who built a port on the Marmara. Valens developed the water supply system, building the aquaduct of Valens (Bozdoğan Kemeri). The main cistern and fountain were built at Beyazit Nymphaeum Maximum). The city thus took on the character of a grand Roman capital, as Constantinopolis.

As the city grew and developed a number of important Forums were built where much civic activity was centred. The most important of these were:

1 - The Augusteon: This was between what is now known as Ayasofya and Sultanahmet mosque. There were several statues and columns adorning the square and in the centre was a Triumphal Gate with a milliarium - milestone monument underneath, symbolising the centre of roads leading to all the provinces of the vast Roman empire.

2 - Forum Constantini: This was in the present area of Çemberlitaş. An oval piazza with double arcades on several levels, it was decorated with statues, and in the centre on a porphyry column stood the figure of Constantine as Helios in the form of a gilded bronze statue. After later cracks appeared in this column, bronze clamp bands were fitted around it, giving it its Turkish name - Çemberlitaş - the banded stone.

3-Forum Tauri (Piazza of the bull): Named after a commander of the guard known as Taurus, it is said that in the centre of the piazza was the bronze statue of a bull. The piazza was restored by Theodosius I, and embellished by a grand bronze statue of the emperor with his hand oustretched towards the city, hence the alternative name of Forum Theodosii.

4 - Forum Amastrianum: This was to the present neighborhood of Şehzadebaşı.

The Hagia Sophia (XIX. century)

5 - Forum Bovis (Piazza of the ox): named after a large statue of an ox-head which had been brought from Pergamon. The piazza was situated on the site of the present Aksaray Piazza.

6 - Forum Arcadi: Named after the emperor Arcadius (395-408 A.D.), it is also known as the Herolophos. Probably rectangular, it had the column of Arcadius in the centre, the marble base of which can be seen today in situ, 100 m. from the Cerrahpaşa mosque. Among the other columns once decorating the square is the so-called Maiden's column erected for the emperor Marcianus by Tatianus (450-457 A.D.) and the Gothic column now on Seraglio Point.

With the addition of these piazzas and columned roads throughout, Constantinopolis took on the character of an imperial Roman city, the columned roads providing protection from the hot summer sun and winter rain.

With the rise of Christianity, the new religion gave the city a new identity, with churches being built on every corner.

After the great schism of 395 A.D. when the Roman empire was divided in two, a new era began for Constantinopolis, as it became the capital of the so-called new Rome, now known as the Byzantine empire.

During the region of Theodosius II (408-450 A.D.) the city underwent further considerable expansion; the walls were extended to the west, and the section between the Marmara Sea and Tekfur Sarayı which survives today was built. To begin with, the new area within the city walls was not entirely built-up. Apart from a number of harbours on the Marmara of various sizes, the city had the advantage of being built on the Golden Horn, which is a harbour in itself. The largest of the harbours on the Marmara was the Langa, which later silted up.

While the main roadways were generally columned, auxiliary roads and streets were narrow, dark passages. Restrictions were placed on housing. Houses, which were stone, were to be built in terraces, to prevent restriction of the view from neighbouring dwellings, and allowing for adequate ventilation. Different streets or neighbourhoods were allocated to artesans, artists and even foreign merchants. There were a great number of churches and monasteries. Meanwhile the Grand Palace was constantly extended to cover an ever-greater area. Other private palaces were built throughout the city, such as the Mangana Palace at Sarayburnu. From the XI century onwards, imperial palaces began to be built in the district of the Blachernai, and the Grand Palace was gradually abandoned. During the XII century, there were large open spaces, fields, orchards and gardens within the city walls. Monastries surrounded by groves of trees dominated the hills of the city. While the monastery buildings were of wood, houses, palaces and churches tended to be of stone, hence the city was much damaged by successive earthquakes, although relatively little effected by fire. The Latin siege of Constantinople in 1203-1204, after which the city was captured by the IV Crusaders, wrought considerable damage to the city. Successive fires resulted in its eventual desertion. During the 60 years of Latin rule following this the city fell largely into ruin.

By 1261, when Constantinople was recaptured by Michael VIII (1261-1282) over half the city was burnt down. The emperor attempted to rebuild it, building new monasteries on the site of the old and re-housing the populace. Although the columned ways were not resored, the city now acquired roads lined with trees. The Bosphorus region, which had not been much settled during the earlier Byzantine are was totally vacated.

Palaces and monasteries outside the city walls were abandoned, in preference for new monastries in the farthest corners of the city, such as Chora, Lips, Studios,

The Obelisk of Theodosius and the Serpentine Column

Panmacharistos, Andreas and others, which were set in their own extensive land in the form of small complexes. At various times in Byzantine history a total of 485 churches and 325 monasteries and convents are known to have existed in constantinople. By the XIV and XV centuries, the city had become considerably impoverished, and was very sparsely populated. Until, in 1453, it was conquered by Mehmet II, after which time it became a Turkish city. During the Ottoman period, the walls and many buildings were restored and new neighbourhoods were developed. Palaces, mosques, hans, baths and fountains were among the newly built monuments which served to give the city a Turkish character.

The largest Christian church in the Ottoman capital of Istanbul, Hagia Sophia was converted, according to tradition, into a mosque soon after the city was taken. A palace was built on the site of the present Istanbul University (Eski Sarayı). Churches continued to be used as mosques throughout the city. Muslims were brought from throughout the Ottoman provinces to resettle in Istanbul, while Christians throughout the empire were given freedom to practise their religion. Genoese and Venetian merchant colonists were given guarantees of their continued rights as citizens. After Mehmet II, the Ottoman throne was occupied by Bayezid II who constructed the Beyazit mosque in the piazza of the same name. In 1509, the city was much damaged by a serious earthquake. Reconstruction took place on a grand scale with a workforce of 80,000 builders. During the reign of Selim I the Ottomans conquered Egypt, Syria and Mesopotamia.

The Ottoman sultans acquired the title of Caliph, Selim I being the first caliph. Many moslem sacred relics were brought from Egypt to Istanbul, including artefacts used by Muhammed the Prophet and his follower. These relics are still preserved in a section of Topkapı Palace.

The city was at its most splendid during the reign of Süleyman I. Belgrade was taken by the Ottomans, who had undertaken successful campaigns to Hungary and Vienna. The Ottoman fleet had turned the Mediterranean into a Turkish lake; the greatest architect of the Ottoman period, Mimar Sinan was also a product of this era. He was to make a lasting mark on Turkish architecture. Among his major works were Şehzade mosque and Süleymaniye mosque. It was a law-making period, when the organisation of the state was formalised, and it was an age of ascendancy for art and philosophy. European travellers of the period, foreign envoys and visiting artists who experienced Ottoman court life at close quarters described it in their works. From the XVII century onwards, the sultan's supremacy began to decline, political power falling into the hands of viziers and dowager sultans. Innumerous works of Baroque and Rococo inspiration in the Turkish style were produced during the XVII and XVIII centuries. Turkish rococco is known as the "Tulip Period".

Throughout the XIX century conflict and struggle were widespread in the Ottoman dominions, which were spread over three continents. The Balkans were struggling for independence, while Russia was in search of access to the sea and ways of dominating the Balkans. The English and French, meanwhile, were bent on protecting their interests in the Near East. By the end of the century, the Ottoman empire was powerless in Europe. By 1912 the Bulgarians were at the gates of Istanbul and in two years time World War I had begun. Istanbul was under British and French occupation in 1918 and the Ottoman caliph fled the coutry in 1922. In 1923 the Turkish Republic was founded and Mustafa Kemal Atatürk became its president, in the new capital of Ankara.

Miniatures

Miniatures

19

SULTAHMET SQUARE THE HIPPODROME

This was built after the Circus Maximus in Rome by Septimius Severus, and construction begun in 203 A.D. Later, during the reign of Constantine I it was vastly enlarged, and completed in 325 A.D. The hippodrome was then horse-shoe in shape, and measured 400 × 120 ms. It could seat 100,000 spectators on 40 rows. Enclosed by high walls, it had tribunes on three sides, and the emperor's loggia on the fourth (the eastern) side. In the centre of the race track was the raised pavement known as the Spina (central line), which was there to keep the traffic in line during chariot races.

Previously there had been a ditch in its place, at a time when the hippodrome had housed games. When chariot races replaced the games, the ditch was filled in and the raised terrace wall built in its place. Columns and statuary from all parts of the empire were set up on the Spina, of which only three monuments now survive. Among the statuary known to have been erected are the figures of a warrior in combat with a lion, a dying bull, the Heracles of Lysippos, a wild horse, an eagle catching a snake, the emperors Gratianus, Valentinian and Theodosius, and the figures of prizewinning charioteers. The statues were of bronze or marble. Over the emperor's loggia, set on two towers stood four bronze equestrian statues, the work of Lysippos, which are now in the piazza of

Mustafa Kemal Atatürk (1881-1938)

The Turkish flag

St. Mark, Venice. They were transported there during the 13 century by the Latins, during their occupation of Istanbul.

As now, the competitors of the races were divided into teams, known as the reds, the yellows, blues and whites, for exam-

The Hippodrome, Sultanahmet mosque, Hagia Sofia museum and the German fountain

ple. These teams were large organisations with their own stables, and stud farms. They had various clubs and organised membership. In time, however, these organisations were attached to the government, and their members became the emperor's official soldiers.

The signal for the games was the white tent of the emperor, which was set up a day before the races. The populace queued outside the gates the night before and were let into the hippodrome the morning of the races. The clubs became so popular that their importance ran beyond the sports field into the field of politics. The well-known Kika insurrection was related to the clubs. Finally, in order to put a stop to such insurrections, the emperor gradually began to cut down the games until finally they were forbidden altogether. The hippodrome then became a parade ground and ceremonial area.

The Latins were responsible for inflicting considerable damage on the hippodrome. The crusading army, on its arrival in Constantinople, salvaged all the metal artefacts they could find to mint much needed money. Among their spoils were the metal statues on the Spina. After the Turkish conquest of Constantinople, the hippodrome was restored to some of its former glory, once again becoming a centre of ceremony and entertainment as it had been earlier in Byzantine times. Around it were built some of the finest Turkish monuments of the era, including the Ibrahim Paşa palace, the Ayasofya baths and the Sultanahmet Mosque. The three original ancient monuments still in situ on the site of the Spina are as follows: **The obelisk of Theodosius (The Egyptian obilisk),** actually ancient Egyptian in origin. Originally erected by Tutmosis III (1504-1450 B.C.) before the temple of

Sultanahmet mosque

Karnak at Heliopolis. It is a monolith, 25 ms. in height in red porphyry. The hieroglyphic inscription it bears describes the victories of the pharaoh. At the tip the pharaoh is seen offering sacrifice to the god Amon-Ra; the pharaoh kneels at the foot of the god. This obelisk was brought to Constantinopolis in 390 A.D. by the Byzantine emperor Theodosius I, and erected over a rectangular stone base on four bronze feet. The marble base in itself is 6 ms. high and is covered with relief carving. The relief on the northern face shows scenes from the erection of the monument. The emperor is seen watching the monument being set in place. The eastern face shows the emperor and his family watching the chariot races. The reliefs on the south face show the imperial family in the emperor's lodge during the games, while on the western face we see the emperor's defeated antagonists prostrated before him. There are two inscriptions beside the reliefs, in Greek and Latin.

Constantine's Column: Although not precisely dated, this is thought to date from the IV century. The monument, which is 32 ms. in height is of sandstone ashlar masonry. It is known that this monument was formerly revetted with gilded bronze plaques. During the Latin invasion in 1204 these plaques were removed, smelted down and minted. They were, however, restored by Constantine VII Porphyrgenatus VII (913-959 A.D.), with the addition of inscription plaques relating the achievements of his grandfather during his lifetime. On the marble inscription on the base of the obelisque it reads:- "Constantine restored this now ruined monument to a state better then the original". Excavations around the base have shown that there were fountains on all four sides of the monument.

The Serpent's Column (Spiral Column): This is one of the oldest monuments in Istanbul. It is part of a larger monument set up to commemorate the victory of 31 Greek cities against the Persians at Salamis and Platae in 479 B.C. Originally the monument was presented to the temple of Apollo at Delphi in the form of a tripod cauldron base, which is known to have been surmounted by a tri-footed golden cauldron. It was cast from Persian weapons gathered as spoils after the Greek victory. The spiral column was in the form of three intertwined serpents, the gold cauldron supported on their heads. Two of these heads survive, one in the Istanbul Archeological Museum, the other in the British Museum. The third is lost. The present column is 5.5 ms. although the original was 8 ms. high. It was probably brought to Istanbul and erected by Constantine.

Sultanahmet mosque (The Blue Mosque): Built by the architect Mimar Sedefkar Mehmet Ağa for Ahmet I, between 1609-1616. Its six minarets are unique. Surrounded on three sides by courtyards with five portals, the portico is covered by 30 cupolas supported by 26 marble columns with stalactite capitals. In the centre of the main courtyard is a hexagonal fountain. The mosque itself has three doors. The largest opens into the main courtyard, and it is this door which is used as the entrance today. The mosque is almost square in plan. The central dome is supported by four marble piers with four arches sprung between. The dome is flanked on all four sides by a semi-dome with cupolas at the corners. The extraordinary height of the dome (23 ms.) allowed for an unusual number of windows (260 in all) which provide the interior with a warm, overall light which illuminates the rich tiling and tracery. According to the sources, there are a total of 21,043 faience tiles, each valued at 18 silver akches.

The sultan's gallery - mahfil - is in the left corner of the mosque, and has a fine mihrab decorated with mosaic and green tiles. The mother-of-pearl inlay door, gild-

Aerial view of Sultanahmet Mosque, Hagia Sofia Museum and The Bosphorus

View of the Sultanahmet mosque by night

ed faience and filigree relief-carved marble balustrades are extraordinarily fine. The mosque, also known as the Blue Mosque, is so-called after the faience revetments. Those on the gallery level are particularly fine. The blue-green faience wallpanels are countered by tracery on the dome in similar tones. The dome is also inscribed with the names of the caliphs. It was from the steps of the marble pulpit - mimber - that Mahmut II declared the dissolution of the Janissary in 1826. The mihrab, also in white marble is decorated with precious stones and a piece of rock from the Ka'ba.

The mausoleum of Ahmet I, founder of the mosque, is situated to the northeast together with those of Osman II and Murat IV. Until the 19 century Sultanahmet mosque was the traditional starting point for the pilgrimage to Mecca.

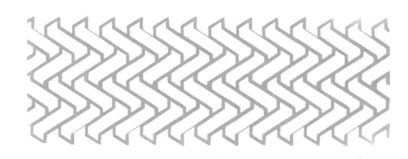

Interior of the Sultanahmet mosque

Sultanahmet mosque

Interior of the dome, Sultanahmet mosque

Stained glass window

THE MUSEUM OF TURKISH AND ISLAMIC ARTS

The museum was founded in 1914. It was the first Turkish museum to possess a comprehensive collection of both Turkish and Islamic artefacts. Housed in the Süleymaniye complex from its foundation up to 1983, in the arms houses - imaret - it moved to the newly-restored Ibrahim Paşa Palace in 1983. The palace, which was restored especially to house the collection, is one of the most important examples of Ottoman civil architecture of the 16 century. Unlike many palaces of the period, it was constructed in stone, rather than wood, which accounts for its survival. It was built on the terraces flanking the ancient hippodrome (At meydani), overlooking the column of Theodosius, the Serpent's column and the spiral column. In 1520, it was restored by Süleyman I and presented to Grand Vizier Ibrahim Paşa in 1520. It was both a vizierate palace and from time to time, an imperial loggia during public ceremonies. Now restored according to the pictorial evidence of 16 century miniatures and the drawings and engravings of western artists, the palace houses a collection of 40,000 objects. The Rug department contains rugs dating from the 7 to the 19 centuries, among them some extremely fine examples. The collection also has a notable manuscript selection, while early stone carving and Seljuk and Ottoman woodcarving are unique. The newly founded Ethnographical section of the museum presents a cross-section of Turkish folk life, with rug and kilim looms; weaving and wool dying techniques shown in the context of their folk environment. On the lower floor, at the entrance of the museum is a row of shops reconstructing an old Turkish bazaar, where gifts and books may be purchased. The museum also has a conference room on this floor. In the courtyard is a typical Turkish coffee house where coffee, tea, salep and sherbet are served.

Museum of Turkish and Islamic Arts

HAGIA SOPHIA

Hagia Sophia: The most renowned Byzantine cathedral and the best-known Christian church in Istanbul. The first church was built between 325-360 A.D. Construction was begun during the reign of Constantine and completed by his son Constantius (337-361 A.D.). Being the largest imperial church in the city it was kown as the Megalo Ekklesia. The name Hagia Sophia (Sacred wisdom) was adopted in the fifth century, and it was by this name that the cathedral continued to be known throughout the Byzantine era, being corrupted in the Turkish era to Ayasofya.

The earliest church is thought to have been a stone-walled basilica with timber roof. This is known to have opened its door to worship with great ceremony on 15 October, 360 A.D. It was burnt down during an insurrection in the V century by an angry populace protesting against the banishment of the bishop of Constantinople, Iohannes Khrysostomos to Arcadius. The bishop, a zealot, was banished for his repeated attacks on the empress. The insurrection took place on 20 June, 404 A.D.

Theodosius II (408-450 A.D.) appointed

Museum of Ayasofya (Hagia Sofia)

Interior of the Ayasofya Museum

Interior of the Ayasofya Museum

Interior of the Ayasofya Museum

the architect Roufinos with the task of rebuilding the church, which was rebuilt as a basilica and opened to prayer on 8 October, 415 A.D. This too was short-lived, the second church being burnt down during the Nika insurrection on 13 January, 532 A.D. Traces of this building can be seen outside the western wall of the present church. They were uncovered during excavations in 1935 at a depth of 2 ms. A flight of five marble steps leading up to a porticus and from there to a narthex through three portals is clearly visible. The church was apparently 60 ms. wide, although further excavation was impossible without endangering the substructure of the present building, so the length is not known.

Justinian ordered a new church built of an unprecedented size and magnificence. He appointed two of the most famous architects of the day to carry out this task - Anthemios of Tralles and Isidoras of Miletus. Only 39 days after the fire which

destroyed the earlier church, work on the new church was begun. After past experience, timber was avoided in its construction. Valuable marbles were brought from all corners of the empire. Columns for the interior were brought from temples at Baalbek, Heliopolis, Ephesus and Delphi, while other pillars and capitals were made of white Proconessos, green Tesselian, golden Lybian, pink Phrygian and ivory Cappadocian marbles. The main walls, the dome, vaults and arches were built of brick. The construction took five years, with 1000 master craftsmen and 10,000 labourers working on site. The new church was opened on 27 December, 537 A.D., with ceremony. Leading the ceremony was the emperor Justinian, who approached the church in his ceremonial coach, and was received by the Grand Patriarch - Menas. They entered the church arm in arm, according to tradition. It is said that the emperor, processing towards the apse, in a state

İnterior of the Hagia Sophia

of great excitement proclaimed his thanks to God or having the honour to have constructed such a magnificent church, and shouted "Solomon, I have surpassed you".

Today, after repeated restoration and additions, the Hagia Sophia is notably altered. Several earthquakes damaged the structure and in 558 A.D. the dome partially collapsed. This was rebuilt by the young Isidoros, when the dome was raised by 6.25 ms., and reopened in 562 A.D. Later repairs failed to provide the building with the static support essential for its stability. Repeated earthquakes continued to weaken the fabric and the cost of maintainance rose continuously. During the Latin invasion, the IV crusaders sacked and damaged Hagia Sophia, as if it were a pagan temple, in 1204. The gilded silver panels flanking the Imperial portal were taken as booty by crusading soldiers, along with gold and silver crosses and any available valuables, while crusading monks acquired what religious artefacts they could, inflicting the greatest damage ever suffered by the cathedral throughout history.

When the city was recaptured by the Paleologs in 1261, the emperor Michael VIII (1261-1282) ordered the restoration of the church by the monk and architect Ruchas. The buttress walls on the western facade date from this period. Pyramidal buttresses were added to the northern and southern walls in 1317 to offset the effect of the dome's weight which was pushing out the walls. This addition dates from the reign of Andronicus II.

On the Turkish conquest of Istanbul in 1453, Mehmet II found the church in a state of ruin. The conqueror lead the first Friday prayers there and ordered it to be converted into a mosque. Later a mihrab was added to the eastern apse in line with the qibla - facing towards Mecca, and a wooden minaret was erected over one of the western cupolas. The main structure and mosaics on the interior were left untouched. Later, during the period of

Fresco of the Madonna and Child from the Ayasofya Museum

Süleyman I (1520-1566) the mosaics were plastered over. The brick minaret on the south-eastern flank and a buttress wall on the eastern facade were added earlier, during the reign of Mehmet II. The slimmer minaret on the north-eastern flank was added during the reign of Bayezid II (1481-1512), while the two more solid minarets to the west were additions of the Selim II (1566-1574) period, and were constructed by the architect Sinan.

The Ottoman sultans restored and maintained the building in the best possible state, embellishing it with Islamic works of art. A muezzin's gallery in fine relief marble was added to the furniture of the mosque during the reign of Murat III (1574-1595). Two marble amphorae dating from the Hellenistic period were brought from Bergama and set up to either side of the portal on the interior, which, with the addition of faucets, were used for ritual washing before prayer. Two large candelabrae flanking the mihrab were among the spoils of Budin, captured by Süleyman I during his Hungarian campaign. A marble mimber and the marble pulpit set to the left of the space under the main dome were added during the reign of Murat IV (1623-1640). A library adjoining the mosque was added during the reign of Mahmut I. Finely decorated with Iznik tiles, it contained space for 30,000 books. During the same period a fountain - one of the finest in Turkish architecture - was erected in the mosque court, together with a school and observatory. Four sultan's mausoleums are to be found in the eastern corner of the gardens which also contain the Baptistry, later converted into a mausoleum.

The most extensive restoration to the fabric of Hagia Sophia took place during the reign of Abdülmecit (1847-   ). Under the direction of the Italian architect Gaspar Fossati, the dome was stabilised by the addition of a double iron band clamped around it. The roof was releaded and columns moving out of true were restored. The mosaics were uncovered and restored, those with cruciform patterns and human figures replastered,

Mosaic portraits of Constantine IX and the Empress Zoe

The Ayasofya Museum

Interior of the dome

while the imperial gallery was given its present day appearance by Fossati. The restorations took two years.

The large inscription plaques, 7.5 ms. in diameter were attached to the walls at that time. They were the work of the calligrapher Hattat Izzet Efendi, who also decorated the dome with his inscription of verses from the Kor'an.

Haghia Sophia was declared a national monument and became a museum by order of Atatürk on 24 October, 1934.

Visiting Haghia Sophia:

The church is entered via the western portal which leads into the Exonarthex, from which five portals open into the Narthex (11 × 60 ms.), notable for the polychrome marble revetments.

The narthex opens into the main body of the church through nine portals, the three central portals being the Imperial Doors. Over the main portal is a mosaic of Christ enthroned dated to the 9th century. The figure of Christ has his right hand raised in blessing, while his left hand holds up a book resting on his knee. The mosaic is flanked to right and left by the figures of the Blessed Virgin and the angel Gabriel in roundels. Prostrated before the throne is the figure of Leo VI (886-912 A.D.).

The total area of the church including its narthexes is 7570 m². It is the fourth largest church in the world. The interior is dominated by a dome 55.60 m² in height. The dome is not quite circular, measuring 30.8 m. × 31.88 m., and rests on four main piers joined by four supporting arches. The drum is pierced by forty windows. Of the surviving decoration, the Cherubim in the pendentives are frescos dating to the 10th century. The mosaic of the Mother of God enthroned, bearing the Christ child in the apse dates to the 9th century. The figure of the Madonna (Theodokos Madonna) is of idealised beauty.

Set within blind niches along the north wall are the mosaic portraits of three beatified members of the church clergy, the Patriarch of Constantinople, Iohannes Khrysostomos, the archbishop of Antalya, Ignatios and St. Ignatios Theophoros, in frontal pose against a gold ground.

In the northern nave is the so-called "sweating column", of pourous marble which absorbed water from a cistern below. The damp absorbed by the column can be felt by placing the hand in a hole in the shaft which has been worn into it and is framed in bronze. Even in Byzantine times this piller was considered miraculous.

At the south of the central nave is an area of marble mosaic of extremely fine quality. This is believed to be the spot upon which the Byzantine emperors were crowned, and was known as the Byzantine omphalos (centre of the earth). The church is surrounded on three sides by galleries, there being no gallery over the apse. The galleries have finely decorated ceilings and contain some mosaics of considerable value.

The Deesis mosaic in the south gallery is dated to the 12th century. It is partially destroyed, but still the fine and delicate workmanship of the mosaic can be easily seen in a work of particularly small tesserae. The figure of Christ is flanked by the Virgin and John the Baptist, on a golden ground.

Set into the wall opposite is the tombstone of Enrico Dandola, Doge of Venice, dated 1205. Further along the gallery in an area reserved for imperial portraits we see two mosaics of note. The mosaic to the left is dated to the 11th century and shows Christ flanked by the Empress Zoe and her third husband, the emperor Constantine IX (1042-1054). To the right is a 12 century mosaic panel portraying the Virgin and child flanked by the emperor Iohannes Comnenos II (1118-1143) and the empress Eirene. Their son Alexios is

Mosaic of the Pantocrator Christ, Ayasofya

portrayed on a narrow panel on the wall to the right. His pale and wasted expression is that of a prince who died in his twenties. From this point the apse mosaic of the Virgin man be seen in detail.

Descending from the gallery via the imperial ramp, one may exit from the southern portal of the narthex. The bronze door here is noticable. The door dates from the Hellenistic era and was brought to Istanbul from a temple in Tarsus. The mosaic over the portal shows the Virgin, standing, with the Christ child in her arms. To her right the emperor Constantinus Magnus offers up a model of the city, while to her left Justinianus proffers a model of the Hagia Sophia.

The gilded tesserae used in the mosaics of the Hagia Sophia were made by spreading gold leaf over a layer of glass tesserae, after which this was finished with a further layer of glass paste. This prevented the gilding from deteriorating.

Mosaics of the Empress Zoe, Madonna and child and the emperor from the gallery of the Ayasofya

Bird's eye view of the Hagia Sophia Museum

General view of Ayasofya

CHURCH OF SERGIUS AND BACCHUS (KÜÇÜK AYASOFYA)

This church was built by the emperor Justinian (527-565) between 527 and 536, and devoted to the saints Sergius and Bacchus. It is a two-storeyed church, with a Turkish narthex added to the western front. Basically centrally-planned, the ground floor is in the form of an irregular rectangle, within which the dome rests on an octagon surrounded by 8 octagonal piers, with two columns between each pier. The space behind the columns forms an exhedra at the corners. Around the curved frame created by piers and columns is an ambulatory. One interesting feature is the existence of an inscription frieze between the ambulatory and the gallery, above the columns. It is one of the rare examples of such friezes in Byzantine architecture. It bears a laudatory inscription concerning the achievements of the Empress Theodora, wife of Justinian.

The Küçük Ayasofya mosque

THE MOSAIC MUSEUM

The Mosaic Museum is to be found in the arcade of shops attached to the complex of Sultanahmet mosque. The arcade was built to provide income for the mosque, but was destroyed by fire in 1908, remaining in ruins for a considerable period after that date. Excavations carried out on the site between 1935-38 by Prof. Baxter revealed the remains of part of the Grand Palace of the Byzantine emperors, which appears to have possessed an extensively arcaded courtyard measuring 86 × 55 ms. The arcade was 8.8 ms. in depth. and paved with mosaic. Further excavations carried out between 1951-54 by Prof. Talbot Rice uncovered mosaics which were set up in a museum in 1953. The mosaics belonging to the palace date from the 4-5 century A.D. They were apparently covered over in the 6 century by marble pavements, and built over in the 7-8 centuries. Later, they were incorporated into the Sultanahmet mosque arcade on the construction of the mosque in the 17 century. The mosaics of the Grand Palace, which are displayed in situ, are made of minute stone tesserae. The ground is of white stone tesserae arranged in fish scale pattern, while the figures are worked in tesserae of red, black, green, brown, blue and yellow stone. The mosaics are extremely tactile in effect. The subject matter is secular, the emphasis on pastoral devices in a genre style. Notable among them are the figures

Interior of the Mosaic Museum

of a lion devouring a lizard, a stag entwined with a snake, a woman giving breast to a child, the combat of a spear-bearing hunter and a tiger, a child feeding a donkey, a young girl carring an amphora, a camel with children mounted on its back with a camel-driver and a monkey picking a banana from the tree.

THE UNDERGROUND CISTERN (YEREBATAN SARNICI)

One of the major problems in ancient cities was how to ensure a water supply during seige. Istanbul possessed a series of large cisterns which were constructed with this in mind. Some were open and others covered in. The latter were either square or rectangular in plan, and were roofed over with brick arches and vaults, supported on stone piers, the Yerebatan Sarnıcı is one of the largest covered cistens of the era in Istanbul. It is situated not far from the court of Haghia Sophia.

Yerebatan cistern

The district is named after it. In the Byzantine era, it was known as the "Basilica Cistern". First constructed during the reign of Constantine I (306-337), this underground cistern was restored and extended by Justinian (527-565). It is 141 ms. in length and 73 ms. in width. There are twelve rows of columns supporting the superstructure, each with 28 columns, a total of 336 in all. The columns are 8 ms. in height and are surmounted by composite capitals. The cistern was renowned for the coldness of the water. A street of houses abutting the walls of Topkapi Palace beside the present Gülhane Park, whose houses were recently restored as tourist pension-dwellings, and whose water was obtained from the underground cistern was named after the cold water fountain there - Soğuk Çeşme Sokak.

CISTERN OF 1001 COLUMNS (BİNBİRDİREK SARNICI)

This is between the districts of Sultanahmet and Cağaloğlu, and is thought to have been built during the reign of Constantine I. It measures 57 ms. × 64 ms. and is approximately 14 ms. in height. Although known as the cistern of 1001 columns, it in fact has only 224 columns. It is enclosed by walls 2.92 ms. thick. The superstructure is a system of vaults and buttress arches. The columns are unusual being composite, ie. two column shafts placed one over the other, which are held together by a metal ring clamp.

Pre-restoration view of the interior of the cistern

Head of Medusa from the Yerebatan cistern

45

THE BATHS OF ROXELANE (HASEKİ HÜRREM SULTAN HAMAMI)

The baths are situated between Ayasofya and the Sultanahmet mosque and are generally known as the Ayasofya baths (hamam). It is among the largest of the baths built by the architect Sinan. They were built by Roxelane, the sultana of Süleyman I, as a source of income for Ayasofya mosque. An iscription over the portal by the poet Şair Hudai indicates that they were built in 1553. The baths, which are double, are arranged along a single axis, male and female sections side by side, one section the mirror-image of the other. The men's baths, which overlook Ayasofya, have a fine portal. The buildings add an interesting texture to the urban fabric, the walls being constructed of distinctive alternating courses of stone and brick. The arcade in front of it is of recent date, being built in place of an earlier arcade which burnt down in 1913. The floors are paved with highly decorative polychrome marble. The baths have been restored in recent years and have recently been employed as a centre for the exhibition of Anatolian rugs.

FOUNTAIN OF AHMET III

This was built by Ahmet III in 1728. It is situated before the Imperial Gate, the main entrance to Topkapi. It underwent restoration in 1936. It is a free-standing monumental fountain surmounted by five cupolas and a broad eaved roof. It is finely decorated with a fountain in the centre of each facade, flanked by a blind niche on either side with a ledge for resting. On each corner was a sebil, or khiosk. The monument is elaborately decorated with intricate motifs, among them devices borrowed from other artistic traditions. As a free-standing monument it is one of the most magnificent Turkish fountains in existence.

Baths of Haseki Hürrem Sultan

HAGIA EIRENE

This church is in the first court of Topkapi Palace. It is one of the earliest Christian churches in Istanbul, although since much altered. It was destroyed by fire during the Nika rebellion, and restored and enlarged by Justinian. Theodosius I convened the second economic counsul here in 381. After a serious earthquake in the 8 century the church underwent extensive restoration under Isaiak Leon (717-741).

On first impression, the plan appears to be basilical, with three naves separated by piers and columns. The upper storey is reminiscent of a cruciform plan, with the western arm of the cross elongated and elipsoid in shape. The church is covered with a domical vault. The cruciform mosaic in the apse dates from the iconoclastic period. The row of columns and arches supporting the gallery was added in the Turkish period, when the church was used for purposes other than worship, first as an armoury and a store for war trophies. Later it became a museum and today is attached to the museum of Ayasofya. The church is used for special exhibitions and occasional concerts. During the Byzantine era, Hagia Eirene was connected directly to the complex of Hagia Sophia. Later, during the Ottoman period, various buildings were erected between the two and Hagia Eirene remained within the walls of the palace.

Church of St. Eirene

TOPKAPI PALACE

After the conquest of Istanbul, Mehmet the Conqueror chose a site on the Forum Tauri (Beyazit square) for his first palace. The so-called "Old Palace" - Saray-i Atık - is referred to in the sources as a walled complex, although no traces of it now remain. It features, however, in some old maps and plans of Istanbul, on the site of the present University of Istanbul main building. It is thought that the walls surrounding the university building follow the original walls of the palace, while the main portal is thought to have been where the present entrance is. Another portal looked out onto Süleymaniye mosque. After the construction of Topkapı palace, the old palace became the abode of the members of the sultan's harem who had lost favour or the wives of previous sultans. At one point it is known to have had a broad eaved Baroque portal. Not

Ceremonial Gate of Topkapı Palace

long after the conquest, Mehmet II began the construction of a new palace at Seraglio Point, which became known as Topkapı Saray after a shore palace near the Cannon Gate (Topkapı) of the sea walls. The walls surrounding the point, which is known as the first hill of the city, were 1400 ms. in length. The old Byzantine sea walls on the Sea of Marmara and the Golden Horn were linked up with land walls enclosing the palace, known as the "Sur-i Sultani", and supported by 28 towers. The main gate was the imperial gate - Bab-i Hümayûn - behind the Ayasofya. The gate was formerly surmounted by a keep which was later removed.

The flanking bays in the gate were also revetted in marble.

The new palace was begun within these walls between 1472-1478, and construction continued throughout successive eras with additions being made right up to the mid 19 century. The palace complex includes lodges, pavilions, state offices, dormitories and barracks and private quarters, a mosque, library and huge kitchen. The last pavilion to be built on the site was the Mecidiye Köşk, which is at present open to the public as a restaurant. Several pavilions and villas in the palace grounds on the point were burnt down during a fire in 1863. All trace of them was lost on the construction of the present railway at Sirkeci.

In the first court, entered through the Bab-i Hümayûn, only two imperial pavilions have survived in good repair.

Topkapı Saray

Key to Plan of the Topkapı Palace Museum

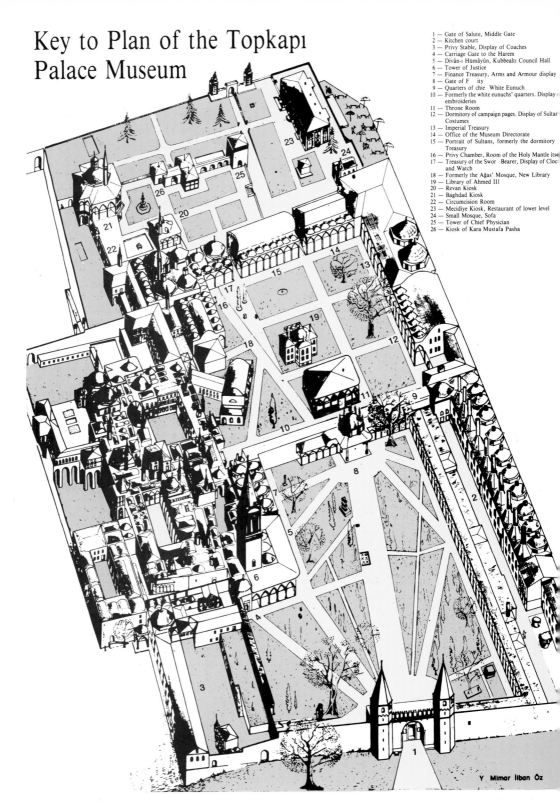

Y Mimar İlban Öz

50

Throne presented to Sultan Ahmet by Nadir Şahin

Harem chambers and the Privy lounge

Topkapı palace became a museum in 1924. It has undergone a number of restorations since then. The first courtyard, also known as the Ceremonial Court - Alay Meydanı, contains, on the right, the offices of the Ministry of Finance - Defterdar dairesi - and on the left, Haghia Eirene, the Ottoman armoury. The road leading to the second gate passes between these two buildings. The second portal, which is flanked by towers, is the Bab-üs selam - the gate of respects, which dated originally from the period of the Conqueror, but which underwent some alterations to the towers during the reign of Süleyman I. During the reign of Mustafa II, a broad eaved bay was added to the inner facade of the portal. Entering through this gate, one passes into the second court which marks the true entrance into the grounds of the so-called Saray-i Cedid - New Palace. On the right of this court are the pantry guards' barracks, the kitchens built by the architect Sinan, the cook's dormitories, a bath, the chief steward's offices and the larder. On the left a road slopes down to the barracks of the Crested Halberdiers and the imperial stables, the livery treasury and the mosque of Beşir Ağa. Further along the court on the left are the double domed chambers which housed the Imperial Council of viziers. This was built by Süleyman I, and it was from here that the state was ruled for a long time. A rectangular tower abuts onto the domed chambers. This was the palace watch tower. It was built in the time of Mehmet I but later altered. The upper storey was timber-built until 1860. The tower was

The Spoonmaker's diamond

Golden helmet

given its present appreance during the reign of Abdülmecid.

The Harem is entered via a door beside the domed chamber, and to the right is the entrance to the imperial records office.

The gate at the other end of the second court, the Gate of the White Eunichs, gives access to the third court, the privy court or Enderun. This gate dates from the reign of Selim III, and has broad eaves. It was under the eaves of this portal that the imperial throne was set during court ceremonies such as those of alliegance, religious celebrations and public audiences. The imperial pennant was erected here too at certain times. The gate was flanked by the chambers and barracks of the White Eunichs.

The third court contained the Throne room. The building dates from the reign of Mehmet II, although the door and decorations date to the 19 century. The overhanging eaves of the building are elongated to cover a columned arcade, and the walls are revetted with faience.

This building was used mainly for imperial audiences to viziers and foreign envoys. Behind the throne room is the library of Ahmet III - Enderün Kütüphane. It is the largest and finest library in the palace. On the right of the court was the Enderun school, artists' and musicians atelier, the barracks of the Campaign Pages, the Treasury, formerly a pavilion in the time of Mehmet II and the remains of a bathhouse dating from the reign of Selim II. On the left of the court is the Treasury

Military Bond in front of the White Euniches Gate

53

The Topkapı dagger

Cradle adorned with diamonds and rubies (XVIII. cent.)

54

of the Sword-bearer - Silahdarağası Hazine - and the apartments of the sacred relics. Further to the left is the vaulted mosque of the white eunichs. The Akağalar mosque has been restored and now houses books and manuscripts collected from all parts of the palace, as the Topkapı Museum Library.

The sultan's privy kitchen is a small building behind the mosque adjacent to the second entrance to the Harem.

Two slightly ramped alleys lead from the third to the fourth courtyard. Flanking the alley to the right is the barracks of the cellar slaves (now the administrative offices of the palace) and the barracks of the treasury guards. To the left of the alley on the left are the chambers of the sacred relics.

The fourth court is a spacious garden, sometimes called the tulip garden - a misnomer based on the word 'lale'. The actual title is the 'Lala's garden'. The chief court physician, or Lala's tower is set on the edge of the terrace overlooking a lower terrace garden. This was the palace

pharmacy. On a terrace wall a little further on from the tower is the pavilion of Mustafa Paşa, also known as the Sofa, which dates to the beginning of the 18 century. It is a fine example of Turkish architecture in an ancient Turkish tradition, decorated with occidental-inspired motifs.

To the left of the court is a stone paved terrace adjoining the chambers of the sacred relics. The terrace extends from the arcade fronting the chambers, and contains an attractive pool. It is reached from the gardens via a short flight of steps abutting onto the Revan pavilion, also called the 'Sevk oda', which was built by Murat IV in 1635. This is an extremely finely decorated pavilion. Manuscripts originally kept in bookcases in the pavilion were later transferred to the museum library. At the end of the terrace on the right, dominating the view of the Golden Horn and the Bosphorus is the Baghdad pavilion, built after Murat IV's second conquest and interior, decorative dome and vaults and mother-of-pearl inlayed

Ceremonial throne of solid gold

Aerial view of Topkapı Palace

doors are among the most striking of its elegant attributes.

At the edge of the terrace overlooking the city and the Golden Horn is a gilded bronze baldachin, which has four fine columns supporting an eaved cupola. Along the eaves runs an inscription frieze containing a long poem which informs us that the baldachin was built by Sultan Ibrahim as a place of vigil. Below it is the fig-grove, or lower garden.

To the left of the terrace, just opposite the chambers of the relics is a small chamber known as the Cicumcision room. This was built by Sultan Ibrahim in 1641, and is decorated with fine tile panels dating to the 16 century but which are reused on this building. The window panels contain small fountains and a long poem is inscribed on the facade.

Two pavilions of note are also to be found on the Marmara side of the fourth court, the 'Çadir Pavilion' and the 'Mecidiye Pavilion', built by Abdülmecit I. The letter is European in style and is the final building to be built in the palace complex. It is flanked by a small wardrobe room - 'esvap oda' and a small chapel mosque with minaret - the Sofa mosque. A path leads down the terrace from the Mecidiye pavilion to a gate which gives access to the outer gardens of the palace, or what is now known as Gülhane Park. A large number of pavilions and royal summer

The Baghdad Pavilion

villas were once to be found in the seraglio gardens, but were burnt down during a fire in 1863, and all trace of them disappeared during the building of the Sirkeci railway which passed through the promontory at this point. Some drawings and plans of these pavilions do, however, exist.

THE HAREM

This is effectively a separate complex within the palace. The main entrance is via the Carriage Gate, dated 1558, from the second court, while there is a second gate - the Kuşhane Gate from the third court and the 'Şal' gate. The carriage gate is flanked by the barracks of the Crested Halberdiers - the sultan's privy guards, and abuts the chambers of the sacred relics on the other side. It is set on a sloping site. Over the 400 years of habitation in the harem, it was added to, restored and changed at various times. It contains 250 rooms, several baths and inner courts. Some of the more notable chambers include the apartments of the Black Eunichs, who were responsible for running the harem, the slaves apartments and hospital, the apartments of the heir elect and the dowager sultan, crown

Crystal jug

Golden jewelry

prices' apartments and the chambers of the favorites. In addition was the sultan's privy chambers, which were a complex in themselves.

Although the harem has not been inhabited by the sultan and his retinue for over a century, it is known that some old court retainers lived in the harem section of Topkapı up to 1908.

The wealth and variety of faience of different periods is one of the most notable features of the Harem.

The museum collection consists of artefacts collected from various parts of the palace, which are now kept in different sections according to their classification. The sections include those of Chinese and European porcelain, arms and armour, costume and carriages, besides the most valuable artefacts in the collection, such as valuable jewellry, encrusted medals and medallions and other artefacts in the precious metals or encrusted with precious stones. Apart from these, the palace also possesses a valuable collection of paintings.

Harem

THE TILED PAVILION - ÇİNİLİ KÖŞK

This is actually within the boundaries of the first court although today it is situated behind the Museum of Archeology in the museum court. Also known as the 'Sirça Saray' - glazed palace, it was built by Mehmet II in 1472. Both the architecture and the decoration of the building are within a Central Asian Turkish tradition. In 1590, during the reign of Murat III, a fountain and pool were added to one of the rooms in the pavilion. The first museum was founded here in 1875. The pavilion is two-storeyed, with a central domed hall and four axial bays, with rooms opening into the corners of the hall. The plan is identical to one also found in Turkish houses. Imposing inscriptions in faience decorate the facade of the building, which is now a pottery and tile museum with a collection of Çanakkale ware.

Çinili Pavilion (the Glazed Pavilion)

THE ARCHEOLOGY MUSEUM

This is one of the most important archeological museums in the world. It was also Turkey's first museum, and possesses, in its collection, a number of unique objects from various past civilisations. Collecting works of fine art is a tradition in Turkey begun during the reign of Mehmet II, who had gathered up various antiques, such as Byzantine imperial sarcophagi uncovered during excavations for the foundations of the Sultan mosque at Fatih. He also collected columns and capitals from Sultanahmet square and the base of the famous sculpture of the charioteers by Porphirius which he had placed in the courtyard of Topkapi Palace, along with other important finds. It was these artefacts which formed the core of the first Turkish museum collection. A similar cicumstance has meant that the entire wardrobes of successive sultans, including their childhood clothes were stored wrapped in cloth. Later, ancient artefacts from all corners of the empire were collected in the church of Aya Irini (Haghia Eirene). In 1876 it was decreed that the Çinili Köşk should be used as a museum. It opened to the public with the title 'Müzei Hümayûn' - Imperial Museum.

As artefacts recovered from various excavations throughout the Ottoman provinces began to increase in number, the

Entrance to the Archeological Museum

Statue of Artemis

present archeology museum building was constructed between 1891-1908. The architect is Valaury. The facade of the building is inspired in form by the famous Alexander sarcophagus and the sarcophagus of the weeping women.

There are twenty large halls on the ground floor and 16 on the first floor. In the lower galleries are displayed examples of Greek, Roman and Byzantine architecture and sculpture, while the first floor galleries are devoted to earthenware, bronze and glassware, mainly small artefacts recovered from various different excavations. There are over 50,000 such items in the collection. In addition there is a numismatic section, with 600,000 coins, medallions and medals which are kept in a cabinet, and an archive of stellae, including 70,000 cunieform tablets. The Treasury section, on the first floor, contains up to 1600 ancient artefacts and pieces of jewellry, and special permission is needed to visit this part of the museum.

The museum also contains a library of 45,000 volumes as an aid to museum researchers.

The most famous rooms in the museum are salon VIII and IX. Salon, which contains the sarcophagi found in the royal tombs at Sidon. These were uncovered during excavations carried out north of Sidon by the founder of the museum, the artist Osman Hamdi Bey in 1887. Considered the greatest archeological discoveries of the 19 century, they were the cause of the museum's foundation.

Sarcophagus

Sarcophagi of various periods were discovered in catacombs of various eras in the two separate caves which constituted the necropolis.

Tomb of the weeping women: Relief carvings of weeping women, each one framed by columns, cover the four faces of the tomb. There are 18 figures in all, some standing, others seated, but all bearing a different expression of grief. The sarcophagus is similar to a Greek temple in appearance, the lid resembling the roof of a temple. On the balustrade around the tomb are represented two separate funeral processions. Originally painted, the colours have now faded. This funereal monument was made for a notable of Sidon in 350 B.C.

Alexander's tomb: This amazing monument is decorated with reliefs on all four sides. On one long side the Greco-Persian wars are represented. Alexander is shown with a lion's pelt over his head, mounted. The artist manages to portray human figures and animals intertwined in combat, with great skill. On the other long face we see the scene of a lion in combat with a stag. There is a battle scene on one, short facade and a hunting scene on the other. This sarcophagus is also in the form of a Greek temple dating from the last quarter of the 4 century B.C. It was originally painted.

The three small sarcophagi at the end of the hall were also recovered from the same tomb. Although undecorated with relief carving, it is plain that they are from the same workshop.

The Satrap's tomb: Three of the four faces of this tomb bear carved relief portraits of a Persion governor - satrap, hence its title. The satrap is shown on one of the long sides on his throne, preparing to go hunting. The opposite face shows a hunting scene. A banquet is shown in relief on one end, and the figures of servants on the other. Although like a Greek temple on the facade, the interior of the tomb is anthropoid. Originally painted, almost all traces of the

Sarcophagus of the Weeping Women, Royal tombs of Saidon

paintwork have now disappeared since the tomb in which it was found was filled with water.

The Lycian Tomb: This has the typical pointed arched lid of Lycian tombs. A lion hunt is shown on one face. Two chariots drawn by four hourses, each containing two youths completely fill the relief. On the other side is the relief of a boar hunt. On the panel at one end two centaurs are engaged in combat with a a Lapith. At the other end is a scene of two centaurs in combat with a stag. In one of the pediments are two addorsed griffins, and on the other are two reversed sphinxes, their wings outstretched.

The Tabnith sarcophagus: The lid is in the form of a mummified figure with Egyptian facial features. On the lower part of the sarcophagus is an inscription in hieroglyphics stating that the tomb is that of Peneftah, an Egyptian general. Below this is an inscription in Phoenician in the words of Tabnith, king of Sidon, cursing any who lay hands on the tomb. It is dated to the early 6 century B.C. The mummified corpse of Tabnith is displayed in a glass case nearby.

Other anthropoid sarcophagi in the hall also originated from the necropolis of Sidon.

Artefacts found in the sarcophagi together with the corpses are displayed in cases along the wall.

Ceramic panel from the gate of Babylon

THE MUSEUM OF ANCIENT ORIENTAL CIVILISATIONS

The building which houses this museum, in the grounds of the Archeological museum, was built in 1883 as the School of Fine Arts. It was later converted into the museum of Oriental Antiquities in 1917. After several alterations and changes to the museum, it was finally opened as a modern museum in 1974, housing one of the most important world collections of antiquities of the Near East. The collection includes pre-classical Anatolian and Mesopotamian works, and artefacts of the pre-Islamic period from Egypt and the Arabian peninsula.

The greater part of the Mesopotamian collection consists of finds made during excavations in the Mesopotamian basin, bordered by the Tigris and Euphrates before World War I. These include finds from Nineva, Nemrud, Tella, Nipur, Abu Habba, Fara, Abu Hatab, Bismaia, Asur, Babylon and others.

The pre-Islamic examples of Arab art, however, were not discovered during excavation, but gathered up by the Governor of Yemen from southern Arabia and brought to Istanbul in circa 1880. These include mostly inscriptions, relief panels, tombstones and votive figurines.

Tle Egyptian collection was built up from artefacts recoved from excavations, donated from private collections or objects accidentally discovered. It consists of objects dating mainly to the early dynasties and the age of Ptolemaios, including stellae, sphinxes, shrines, sarcophagi and objects from tombs and temples. The sphinx, a composite human

Figurine of Eros in flight

Embroidered prayer rug (early 17th century)

headed lion was to be found guarding the entrance to Egyptian temples, flanking a ceremonial way or monumental gate. They represented the semi-deified figure of the monarch. The finest examples of Egyptian relief are stellae. Egyptian sarcophagi are anthropoid - in human form - and made of wood. They are elaborately painted. These sarcophagi were found in the necropolis of Teb during excavations carried out by the French. They contain the mummies of the priests and priestesses of the temple of Amon.

The collection of Anatolian artefacts was built up from various excavations carried out before World War I. They include artefacts of the Early Bronze Age, dating from the Hatti, those of the high Bronze age, from the age of Assyrian colonisation in Anatolia, early Hittite, the Hittite empire and the late Hittite principalities. There are also artefacts from the Urartian civilisation, from eastern Anatolia and beyond, the mountainous kingdom of the Urartu, dating from the Ist millenium.

THE IMPERIAL LOGE (ALAY KÖŞKÜ)

This is actually within the boundaries of the first court, but is situated at the entrance of what is now a public park, Gülhane Park, once part of the palace grounds.

The Loge was built during the reign of Mahmut II (1808-1839) in typical composite Baroque and Empire style. It was from here that the sultan watched the ceremonial march-past. Over the window arch overlooking the street is an inscription in prose, inscribed by the calligrapher Hattat Izzet Efendi in gilded metal characters on black stone. The building contains an ethnographical collection.

Ceremonial Pavilion (Alay Köşk)

THE BURNT COLUMN (ÇEMBERLİTAŞ)

This column was brought to Istanbul by the emperor Constantine I (306-337 A.D.) from the temple of Apollo in Rome, who had it erected in the centre of the piazza bearing his name - the Forum Consantini. Originally 57 ms. in height, the column had 10 pieces of red porphyry joined together to form a shaft over a massive base. The join between sections of shaft was decorated by a laurel frieze in relief. Surmounting the column was the bronze figure of Constantine as Apollo. Today there are only six porphyry sections to the columns which is only 34.80 ms. According to legend, a number of artefacts sacred to Christians and other religions is said to be buried within the base. Among these legendary objects was said to be a wooden statue of Athena from Troy, the magic staff of Moses, Noah's axe and the seven (five?) pieces of loaf said to have been blessed by Christ. The origin of this folk legend is suggested to be an attempt to prove a link between Christianity, pagan religions and Judaism through the collection in one place of objects believed sacred to one or other of those persuasions.

The burnt column and Nuruosmaniye mosque

The first restoration of the column took place during the reign of Theodosius II (408-450 A.D.) when iron bands were clamped around it to hold the pieces of shaft in place. The bronze statue of Constantine was demolished during a storm in 1105, which caused considerable mortality. Manuel I (1143-1180) replaced the statue with a white marble capital surmounted by a gilded cross. The column was much damaged by a fire in 1779. Abdülhamit I (1773-1789) then had the base enclosed in a wall and the present iron bands fixed to the column. Later, the column became known as the banded column - Çemberlitaş.

THE FIRE TOWER OF BEYAZIT

Mahmut II (1808-1839) first built a wooden observation tower in the grounds of the old palace which was burnt down by the Janissary even before it had been used. The sultan then reorganised the fire brigade and rebuilt the warning tower, this time in stone. An inscription on the base of the tower giving the date of its construction is the work of the calligrapher Hattat Yesarizade Izzet Efendi. The tower was surmounted by a conical wooden roof. In 1850, the present three layered roof was built in place of the earlier wooden roof. One of the architectural landmarks of the city, this white stone tower is European in style. Restored in 1889, it was again damaged during an earthquake in 1894. It is 85 ms. high.

Fires were relatively rare in the city during the Byzantine period since buildings were mainly of stone. But after a major earthquake during the reign of Bayezid II (1481-1521), which inflicted major damage on the city, the citizens chose to build in wood out of fear of further damage. This led to an increase in fires.

The Fire tower, Beyazıt

NURUOSMANİYE MOSQUE

The mosque was begun during the reign of Mahmut I (1730-1754), in 1748. On the death of that sultan in 1756, it was completed by his successor Osman III (   ), and given the name 'nur-i Osmani'. The effects of occidental influence, which began to dominate Ottoman art from the mid-18 century onwards, are clearly seen in this mosque, which is an adaptation of the Baroque to a Turkish architectural genre. It is also the forerunner of monumental buildings indicating the acceptance of a new aesthetic in the Ottoman capital. The mosque, which is rectangular, rises over a high substructure to a single dome. The dome measures 25.75 ms. in diameter. A broad inscription frieze surrounding the interior is within the Turkish tradition. The mihrab is set in a raised niche. In the court to one side are auxiliary buildings including a fountain - sebil, a medrese and mausoleum - türbe, as well as a library containing a valuable collection of manuscripts. The portal to the court opens out into the entrance to the Grand Bazaar. One notable feature of the mosque complex is the ramped entrance to the imperial lodge - Kasri Hümayûn and the imperial gallery.

Nuruosmaniye mosque

THE COVERED BAZAAR

This is the largest covered market in Istanbul. It was originally founded by Mehmet II in 1461 in order to provide traders with a safe and orderly place in which to do their daily business. The market was enlarged during the reign of Süleyman I and finally rebuilt to the present plan in 1701. There are a total of 65 streets within this market, which is a covered area totalling 30.702^2 ms. It is surrounded by a large number of hans -trading inns, which have access to the interior of the bazaar, making them a part of it. Each of these deserves separate notice. Today, the covered bazaar contains a mosque, a mescid - chapel mosque, 21 hans, 2 bedestans (where the valuables wer) kept and sold) 7 fountains, one well, 1 sebil-fountain, one şadirvan - free-standing fountain - and 3300 shops. It possesses a total of 18 portals, eight of these grand portals, others small gates. The doors are closed at 7 p.m., and approximately 50 guards patrol the bedestan throughout the night. Before electricity, the bazaar was lit by huge oil lamps.

The Arab traveller Ibn Battuta, visiting Istanbul with a Kipchak caravan sent by the Kipchak Başbug Özbey Han mentions the existance of a market in the area of the Grand Bazaar almost a century before the Turkish conquest of the city.

The Grand Bazaar

The Bazaar was burnt down five times, the most serious damage was inflicted during the fires of 1546 and 1651. An earthquake in 1894 and fires in 1954 which destroyed more than half the bazaar damaged the traditional features of the structure.

The two bedestans of the Bazaar are known as the Sandal Bedestan and the Cevahir Bedestan.

1. Sandal Bedestan: I. Also known as the New Bedestan, was built by Mehmet II. It is supported in stone piers and had four doors which were closed 50 years ago. The interior of these vaults were arranged in sections for use as an auction room by the town prefect - Şehremini - Cemil Topuzlu in 1914, for the sale of antiques, rugs and jewellry.

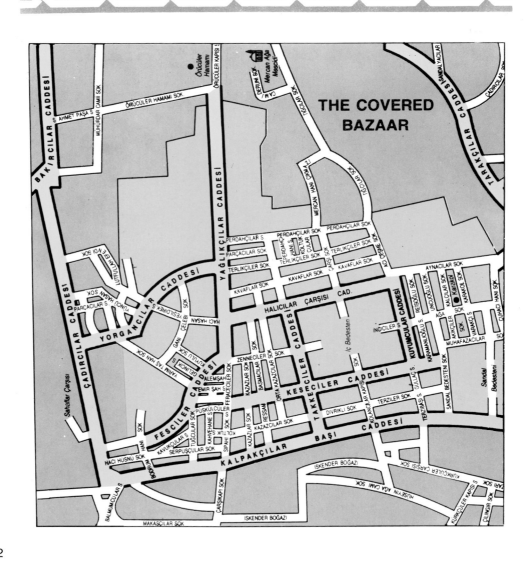

2. Cevahir Bedestan: The İç or inner vaults, also known as the old bedestan, it was reserved for the sale of antiques. It was constructed over walls dating from the Byzantine period, and is covered by vaults and cupolas supported by 8 piers. The total area is 1336 m². During the Ottoman period, jewellers or members of the populace could store valuables here in large iron trunks which were under the shops. These were replaced by safe deposit boxes when banks came into being.

During the Ottoman period, valuable artefacts, fabrics, furs weapons and rugs were bought and sold in the Bedestan. Hence it constituted a merchantile treasury. Now restored, the bedestan has been provided with more light.

Carpet seller in the Grand Bazaar

Shops in the Grand Bazaar

Shops in the Grand Bazaar

THE SÜLEYMANİYE MOSQUE AND COMPLEX

This complex is one of the finest examples of Islamic architecture. It includes 6 medreses, a poor house - tabhane, an imaret - soup kitchens, a caravanserai, mental hospital - bimarhane, baths, a school and shops, as well as the mausoleums of Süleyman I and the sultana Hürrem Sultan (Roxelane).

It was built between the years 1550-1557 by the architect Sinan for Süleyman I (1520-1566).

The mosque has four minarets, two of them have two galleries - şerefe, the other two have three, a total of ten şerefes. This is said to symbolise the fact that Süleyman I was the tenth sultan in the Ottoman dynasty. The mosque is 69 × 63 ms. and has a central dome 53 ms. in height, and 27.25 ms. in diameter. There are 32 windows in the drum. The dome rests on four grand piers connected by four arches. The piers are monolithic porphyry. The dome is flanked by two semi-domes to east and west, and the two auxiliary naves and their galleries are covered by five cupolas of various sizes.

The mihrab and mimber of the mosque, which are of white marble, are particularly noticable. The stained glass windows in the mihrab wall are original (ie 16th century). The faience revetment surrounding the mihrab, and mother-of-pearl and ivory inlayed doors of the mosque are

Süleymaniye mosque

rare works of art. The decoration of the mosque is restrained and balanced, without a hint of exaggeration.

The court is surrounded by a cupolaed arcade where one may see 24 white marble and red granite columns from the hippodrome supporting the 28 cupolas. A rectangular fountain stands in the centre of the inner court.

A bronze grill encloses the nave on the left of the mosque which was converted into a library.

The mosque and its annexes were built with materials brought from great distances as well as from older buildings within the city. One of the piers was brought from Baalbek, another from Alexandria, a third from the court of the old palace and the fourth from Fatih,

Stained glass window, Süleymaniye mosque, detail

Interior, Süleymaniye mosque

where it is known to have been dismantled while in situ.

East of the mosque stand the mausoleums of Süleyman I and the sultana Roxelane (Hürrem Sultan). The tomb of Süleyman, the work of the architect Sinan, is an octagonal domed building. 8 porphyry columns support the dome. The tomb is finely decorated with polychrome faience and stained glass. Some inscribed stones on the eave of the tomb were discovered in 1959 to have been part of a stone-carved inscription from Haghia Sophia, part of the royal decree of the Byzantine emperor Manuel I.

Close to the Süleymaniye mosque is the humble tomb of the great architect Sinan. In the words of one Turkish writer, the tomb is set like a small signature in the corner of a grand oil painting.

Night view of the Süleymaniye Mosque

RÜSTEM PAŞA MOSQUE

One of Sinan's finest works, apart from his imperial complexes, was the mosque of Grand Vizier Rüstem Paşa. The mosque is situated in the trade centre of the old city. Tahtakale. Although there is no inscription giving the construction date of the mosque, a foundation document indicates that it was built in around 1561. As a mosque, both the structure and the decoration render it one of the finest works of Ottoman art. The architect, concerned that the mosque should not be lost .

among the market buildings, raised it up on deep vaults in a most innovative way, and the vaults were used as shop space. There is no large court fronting the mosque, which is reached via flights of steps. The central section of the mosque is surmounted by a large dome flanked by four semi-domes and supported by eight piers. Galleries flank the main area. The minaret was destroyed in 1964. The interior is covered with exquisite tiles from Iznik and Kütahya. Rüstem Paşa also built a han (Çukurhan) close to the mosque and a medrese on the slope leading up to the Süleymaniye mosque.

Faience of Rüstem Paşa mosque

Entrance to the Rüstem Paşa mosque

THE SPICE MARKET (MISIR ÇARŞISI)

This is Istanbul's second covered market. The present structure was built by Harice Turhan Sultan, dowager sultan and mother of Mehmet IV or a part of the foundation of Yeni mosque. According to the documents, the building was begun by the architect Kasim Ağa, and completed together with Yeni mosque by the architect Mustafa Ağa in 1660. It is 'L' shaped in plan. The present structure was last restored in 1943, when the raised wooden counters of the old shops were removed and replaced by modern shop fronts. Apart from six spice shops, the present market has lost its originality.

Spice Market

The structure is of dressed stone with alternating brick courses which both acted as reinforcement and lended the surface of the building an attractive exterior. Stone finials surmount the dome, while details such as mouldings and gutters are fine examples of such details in Ottoman architecture.

The market has six gates and 86 shops. Three of the gates have porticos, giving the building some visual articulation. The mosque and bazaar were formerly contained within sea walls which were later demolished to make way for a road.

Souvenir shops in the Spice Bazaar

Spice sellar in the Spice Bazaar

THE YENİ MOSQUE

This is the last of the great classical mosque complexes. It is built beside one of Istanbul's major quays. Also known as the 'Valide mosque', its title as 'Yeni' or New mosque, was used as a convention in accounts of every period to describe the latest mosque built. The only mosque to have retained that title has been the Valide mosque. The construction was begun by the architect Davut Ağa, for the dowager sultan Safiye Sultan, Mehmet III's mother. On the death of the architect

some time later and that of Mehmet III, Safiye Sultan fell from favour and was sent to the old palace. The construction was then stopped. There was then a long hiatus in the building of the mosque, which had hardly risen above foundation level. In 1660, the dowager sultan of the time, Turhan Sultan saw the unfinished mosque during a visit to the district which had been almost destroyed by fire. She then decided to finish the building and commissioned the architect Mustafa Ağa to do so. Work was completed between 1661-1663. Next to the mosque he constructed the renowned spice market and a splendid fountain and refreshment

The New Mosque

khiosk, together with the mausoleum of Turhan Sultan and other buildings which have since been demolished.

The mosque was built over raised foundations and has two minarets each with three galleries. It is approached by flights of steps, owing to the height of the basal structure. The mosque follows the basic plan of Sultanahmet and Şehzade mosques, with a central dome flanked by four supporting semi-domes. The main dome is 17.50 ms. in diameter and 36 ms. in height. Although classical in style, the proportions of the building are somewhat distorted, the dome appearing a little more pointed than in other mosques. The faience decoration of he mosque is notably fine.

One of the most notable features of the mosque is the imperial lodge - Hünkâr Kasrı. Set on a site overlooking the Golden Horn and the Bosphorus, it is a unique example of classical Ottoman civil architecture. It is connected to the sultan's prayer gallery inside the mosque. Although some valuable tiles were stolen from the mosque, the lodge still retains architectural and ornamental integrity.

With the opening of two important roads to the front and rear of the mosque, the court was demolished.

View of the New Mosque and Galata Bridge by night

THE AQUADUCT OF VALENS

The construction was begun by Constantine I, and completed in 378 A.D. during the reign of the emperor Valens. It links the third and fourth hills and brought water from Alibeyköy to the Nympheum Maximum at Beyazit (in the present University Main Building grounds) which from there went directly to the imperial palace. During the Turkish period, the same water system was used to carry water to Topkapı Palace.

The structure is based on two rows of arches, one surmounting the other. It is known to have been linked to a system 1000 ms. in length, although today only 800 ms. of aquaduct remains intact. 130 ms. of it was demolished in 1509 when the Şehzade mosque was built. Another section to the north west destroyed during urban replanning in 1912.

Two small Byzantine churches are situated south east of the aquaduct. These churches, both of which are now mosques, are known for their mosaics, dating to the 8 and 9 centuries. They are the Kalenderhane mosque and the Kilise mosque.

Aquaduct of Valens and the alley of Haşimişcan

ŞEHZADE MOSQUE

Built in commemoration of the Crown Prince Mehmet, son of Süleyman I, it is one of Sinan's earliest works. It was built between 1545-1548 to a square plan, with a large central dome flanked by four semi-domes. The dome is supported by four arches resting on four piers, and four corner cupolas. The drum has 24 windows. The court is surrounded by an arcade covered with 16 cupolas, linked together by arches supported by 12 columns. The structure and style of the mosque are totally innovative, employing features then as yet unknown in the Ottoman capital. It portents the structural perfection aimed at by Sinan in mosque architecture. To the left of the mosque stand auxiliary buildings in the complex, such as a medrese, poor house and soup kitchens. Just behind the main street wall stand the tombs of the crown princes. That of Şehzade Mehmet is highly decorated. It also contains the tomb of his brother Cihangir. Mehmet was Süleyman's favorite. His early death prevented him from acquiring the throne of the Ottoman empire, which would have been his right. A small model of the throne rests on his tomb. The stonework and faience of this building are extremely intricate and delightful.

Şehzadebaşı mosque

THE FATİH MOSQUE AND COMPLEX

This was the first great Turkish complex to be built on an urban scale in the city after the conquest. The patron was Mehmet (Fatih) (1451-1481) himself. The architect is known as Atik Sinan, with which lakab - pseudonym-he is generally distinguished from Koca Sinan, the great classical architect. Construction of the complex took place between 1463-1470. Architecturally it is one of the most well-integrated and successful groups of buildings of its type on that scale. Among the auxiliary buildings were a school, library, hospital, caravansaray, imaret and hamam, little trace of which however survives today.

The site of the mosque was originally that of a church (Hagion Apostolon) during the Byzantine period, and the site of the imperial cemetery. Excavations carried out during the building of the mosque revealed the tombs of the emperors, which were transferred to the courts of Topkapı Palace and are now in the Archeological museum.

Fatih mosque

A French traveller visiting Istanbul in about 1540, Nicolas de Nicolay) records the splendid appearance of the mosque and the fact that it had an annual income of 60,000 Ducats. The writer also mentions the existance of lodgings around the mosque for the imam and other members of the clergy, as well as hundreds of dwellings in the vicinity set aside for visitors to the city of every race and religion free of charge. When built, the complex covered 10 kms² which made it the largest complex in existance in the city. Much of it was destroyed during a serious earthquake in 1766. The mausoleum was first restored by Mustafa III (1767-1771). The mosque itself was altered some time later to take on its present form. The architect of the present building was Mehmet Tahir. The new mosque was opened to prayer on 15 April 1772.

The frontal court of the mosque is original, as are the faience panels over the windows of the mosque. The court is surrounded by a columned arcade, in which 18 granite columns support 22 cupolas. The main dome of the mosque is flanked by four semidomes and four cupolas flanking them. The main dome rests on arches separated by four piers. The earliest plan of the mosque is not altogether certain, although we way gain some idea of how it may have been from the sources, among them some illustrated. There appears to have been a large central dome with a semi dome on the mihrab wall and three cupolaed sections on the flanking walls.

The paired minarets, each with one gallery, of the original mosque were preserved during the restoration, only to have a second gallery added during the 19 century.

Contained in a cemetry behind the mihrab wall are the tombs of Mehmet I and the sultana Gülbahar. Flanking these to either side were medreses and other auxiliary buildings which have since been demolished or changed beyond recognition.

MİHRİMAH SULTAN MOSQUE

The mosque was built by the architect Sinan for the daughter of Süleyman I, also the wife of the Grand Vizier Rüstem Paşa, Mihrimah Sultan (d.1557). It is in Edirnekapi. Although there is no inscription on the building it is typical of 16 century mosques, having a court linking a medrese with the mosque. It is known to have had a market containing 60 shops attached to the complex, of which certain vaulted arches can now be seen. There is a bath-house close to the mosque. Both the mosque and the medrese were much damaged by earthquakes in 1719 and 1894, after which the minaret was restored quite badly. A single domed mosque, fronted by a portico with seven cupolas, the dome is flanked by sections with three cupolas on either side. The main load-bearing arches bear curtain walls and windows open into them. Light filtering through the stained glass of these windows plays over the decoratively traced interior of the mosque delightfully. The dome is 37 ms. high.

The mosque is quite close to the city walls and the Edirne Gate which was destroyed during an earthquake in 1894 and has since been restored.

THE MOSQUE OF SULTAN SELİM (YAVUZ)

This was built during the reign of Süleyman I in honour of his father Selim I, and was constructed between 1520-1522. It stands on the summit of Istanbul's fifth hill. It possesses a simple rectangular plan, is single domed with a courtyard surrounded by a columned arcade, 18 columns supporting 22 cupolas. There is some doubt as to the identity of the architect of this mosque. Although Evliya Çelebi claims it as a work of Sinan, this seems unlikely. The dome measures 24 ms. in diameter. Among the most notable features of the mosque are its faience and other decorative features.

The cemetery to the east of the mosque contains the mausoleum of Selim I (1512-1520), together with those of various crown princes and sultans, the most recent addition being the mausoleum of Sultan Abdülmecit. Buildings auxiliary to the mosque were later demolished. It seems clear, however, that the complex was originally not extensive.

800 ms. to the east of this church, overlooking the Golden Horn is the so-called Gül mosque, originally the church of Theodosia. This cruciform 10 century church may be visited.

The Yavuz Sultan Selim Mosque

KARİYE (ST SAVIOUR IN CHORA)

This monastery church was built outside the city walls during the 4 century by Constantine I, 'Chora' being Greek for the countryside. It remained within the walls later built by Theodosius II (408-450 A.D.). Much damaged by a serious earthquake in 558 A.D., it was subsequently restored by Justinian (527-565 A.D.), but retained its original name.

It suffered some damage during the iconoclastic period. Being in near-ruin during the 9 and 10 centuries, there is little information about the church to be gleaned from the sources of the time.

The present building, a dome on four piers, was built by the mother-in-law of Alexius Komnenos (1081-1118), Maria Dukania, and devoted to Christ. Later alterations included the addition of several other buildings.

The church avoided occupation during the fourth Crusade in 1204, remaining in the hands of the Orthodox monks. During the reign of Andronikos II

Kariye Museum (St. Saviour in Chora)

(1282-1328), the Grand Logothetes (Chief Minister of the Treasury) Theodoros Methochides, who lived in the vicinity had the building thoroughly restored. A sage and philosopher, he devoted his entire fortune to the restoration of this church and monastery. He added an exonarthex and parekklesion to the building, which are decorated with the finest mosaics and frescos. The mosaics in the exonarthex and narthex and the parakklesion frescos are dated to between 1305-1320.

On the accession of Andronikos Paleologos III (1328-1341) Methochides fell from favour and was exiled. The emperor took over the church and monastery, confiscating the entire fortune of the Logothetes. On his return from exile, Methochides led the life of a simple monk in the monastery. On his death he was buried before the door to the inner narthex.

Chora remained in use as a church for sometime after the Turkish conquest, being converted into a mosque by Beyazit II (1481-1512). Today it is preserved as a historical monument, owing to the valuable mosaics and frescos. The mosaics were cleaned and restored by the American Byzantine Institute.

The present church is flanked by an exonarthex and narthex to the west, the funereal chapel (pareclesion) to the south and a gallery to the north.

THE MOSAICS

The mosaics in the nave at the apse include on the left wall, Christ, a standing figure, with the inscription: "Come unto me all ye that are burdened with suffering"; on the right is the virgin holding the Christ child. In this mosaic, the figure of the Virgin bears the title "Chora touakhoritou" - "place of the supreme", referring to Christ.

Over the door to the narthex from the nave (naos) is the Dormition (Koimesis) of the Virgin. The Virgin lies on her bier

Mosaic of Christ

Christ and his Apostles (mosaic)

surrounded by the apostles. In the centre stands Christ ready to bear her soul to heaven. Her soul is represented by the figure of a new born babe. The figure of Christ is surrounded by a nimbus. Buildings in the background break up the monotony of the surroundings. The narthex vaults and tympanum walls are decorated with gilded mosaic. Above the door to the nave from the narthex is a mosaic of Theodoros Methochides presenting a model of the church to Christ. The figure of the Logothetes, wearing a caftan-like robe and large turban-like headgear kneels in reverence before Christ.

The mosaic in the two domes of the narthex contain mosaics related to the geneology of Christ, portaying his ancestors, beginning with Adam. The life cycle of the Virgin takes up the walls of the narthex. The cycle begins with the Annunciation to St. Anne, in which an angel announces to Anne that she is to bear a child, and ends with the Annunciation to the Virgin that she is to bear the Christ child. The life cycle of Christ follows in the exonarthex.

The Deises, the largest mosaic panel in the church is situated on the wall on the right of the narthex. It shows the figure of Christ with the Virgin on his right but unusually, no John the Baptist on his left. On the left of the panel is the figure of St. Maria with her hands outstretched in supplication of mercy for Mankind. At her foot is the figure of a kneeling prince. Behind this figure is inscribed the name of Isaakios Komnenos (Isaac Commenus) who was the son of Alexius Comnenos

Madonna and Christ (mosaic)

I. On the right stands Melania, queen of the Mongols, dressed as a nun.

Over the door to the narthex from the exonarthex is the mosaic of Christ Pantocrator. The figure is given the title "Shora ton zonton" which links the name of the church with a reference to "the land of the Living". The Christ figure holds the Bible in his left hand and with his right hand blesses the faitful as they enter the church.

Apart from the two figures of saints and the figures of the Virgin and John the Baptist on the soffits in the other narthex, the entire exonarthex is devoted to the life cycle of Christ.

On the lunettes of the narthex (the tympanum walls) is the cycle of the Infancy of Christ, in the vaults is the Ministry of Christ, including his Baptism and Miracles.

The Pareclesion is the funerary chapel on the south side of the church. Being a place of burial, the more humble medium of fresco has been chosen to decorate the chapel in place of mosaic. It is more restrained than the church in decoration. The Pareclesion is 5 ms. wide and 16 ms. long. It is a two sectional building, the burial place is a rectangular, domed area, flanked by niches to right and left within which were the tombs of Byzantine notables. A fresco of the Virgin and Child decorates the dome. The Virgin is surrounded by guardian angels.

In the apse is the Anastasis (Resurrection), in which Christ, within a nimbus, holds Adam and Eve by the hand as they are raised from their tombs. To his right stand the apostles and to his left the saints. Beneath the feet of Christ lies Satan, prostrate and bound with chains. The main vault of the church is the Last Judgement and the second coming of Christ. Christ sits in judgement in the centre with the Virgin to his right and John the Baptist to his left pleading for mercy for Mankind. One of the most important features of the fresco is that it is the first such representation, in a 14 century

Fresco showing Adam and Eve in ascension

church, of a large group of naked people. The walls of the Pareclesion are decorated with figures of the military saints, which illustrates the popularity of such saints during the last years of the empire. Perhaps if the Byzantine rulers had not entrusted the security of their city quite so much to the saints, the empire would have prevailed a little longer.

Sleeping Madonna (mosaic)

Kariye Museum (St. Saviour in Chora)

93

Sherbet seller in front of the German Fountain

YEDİKULE

This is a fortress on the Byzantine land walls near the Marmara. It is now preserved as an historical monument, and is open to visitors as a museum.

Theodosius I (379-395 A.D.) built a triumphal portal here at Yediküle, opening onto the road to the imperial palace. The "Porta Aurea" or 'Golden Gate' as it was known, was a monument to the victory of Theodosius against Maximus. Byzantine historians claim that the portal was surmounted by a statue of Theodosius and four elephants. These statues were demolished during earthquakes in the 8 and 9 centuries. Flanking the triple arched portal are two rectangular towers (pylon). The portal itself is 20 ms. high, and is constructed of white dressed marble. It was called the 'Golden Gate' as both the gate panels and the towers were decorated with gilding. During the building of the Theodosian walls in 413 A.D., the Golden Gate remained within the walls and another portal, the "small golden gate" was built into the new walls. On the building of further reinforcements in 447 A.D. around the city, this too was taken within walls.

Originally there was a fortress of seven towers here during the Byzantine period, two more towers being added later. Known in Greek as "Heptapygion", the present Turkish name is a direct translation of the original "Seven Towers". It was in ruins by the Turkish conquest, but was restored by Mehmet II in 1457-8. During the Ottoman period, the Ottoman treasury was stored there, and in later

The Tekfur Palace, Yediküle

years it became used as the state prison. A gate flanking the eastern tower gives access to the fortress court, which is pentagonal. The remains of an Ottoman mosque may be seen in the court. Opposite are the walls of Theodosius II and the Golden Gate. The eastern tower is also known as the 'inscribed tower' as the interior walls are covered with inscriptions. These were written by foreign envoys imprisoned in the fortress during the Ottoman period. A flight of steps leads to the battlements. Beyond the golden gate is a small court and the 'small golden gate'. State executions were carried out on the lower storey of the southern tower flanking the gate. The heads of the executed are said to have been thrown into the 'bloody fountain'. The young sultan Osman II was strangled to death here on the upper storey by the Janissary in 1622.

THE GOLDEN HORN

This gulf, 7 kms. long, has long been a natural harbour of the city. It is as wide as 800 ms. in places, with water 35 ms. deep on average. The rivers of Alibey and Kağıthane, which flow into the Golden Horn, were, like the Göksu and Küçüksu tributaries flowing into the Bosphorus, country resorts much frequented by the citizens of the old town, and the sultans. The Horn itself was the favoured meeting of the sweet waters. 18 and 19 century European travellers have much recounted the forms of Turkish recreation enjoyed at Kağıthane. In the last century the Golden Horn became silted up through erosion, although efforts are now being made to clear out the gulf and to prevent further pollution.

Aerial view of the Golden Horn

EYÜP

An important district on the Golden Horn, Eyüp, it is notable for the vast numbers of cemetries, tombs of the Ottomans, for its fountains, baths, mosques and minarets. It is the most popular centre of pilgrimage in Istanbul, with the mosque considered the most sacred among Moslems flanking the mausoleum of Abu Turkish conquest of Istanbul, Mehmet II's own mentor saw the site of Ersari's grave in his dream. Soon afterwards the site was found and excavated, on royal command, and the grave found. A mausoleum and mosque were immediately erected on the site, approximately 700 years after his death. The original mosque, dating from 1458, was enlarged by Murat III in 1591. Ahmet III (1703-1730) replaced two of its minarets

The Eyüp Sultan Mosque

Ayyub Ansari, standard bearer to the prophet, whose name it bears. Ansari was killed during the Arab siege of Constantinople (672-679). In 1453, after the throne, always underwent an investiture ritual here at this mosque after their enthronement. According to tradition, a Mevlevi sheyh invested each new sultan with the sword of his ancestor, the first Ottoman sultan Osman I (1288-1326). Today the mosque is the centre of pilgrimage for boys who are to be circumcised. The visiting pilgrim also prays before the tomb of Ansari, which is decorated on the interior with the finest faience, some of which are blue and white tiles from the ceramic workshops founded by the Ottomans at Tekfur Sarayı. The tomb is enclosed behind a silver grill. The mosque courtyard is always replete with pilgrims, particularly on Fridays. The mosque is set in a large graveyard, containing the tombs of many great poets, soldiers and statesmen from all parts of

and in the 1800's the mosque was raised to foundation level and rebuilt by Selim III.

The Ottoman sultans, on aquisition of the the empire, and those of the sultans themselves. Walking through the tombs behind the mosque, one may take a path through the centre of the graveyard which will lead to the top of a hill overlooking the Golden Horn. Here is the historical café of Piyer Loti. 'Piyer Loti' (1805-1923) a French writer living in Istanbul, frequented this café, which affords a fine view of the Horn. His drawings and writings decorate the walls of the wooden coffee house.

On the opposite shore of the Horn is a dock dating from Ottoman times, at Kasımpaşa. The Tershane Palace which was behind this shipyard has now disappeared, but for a lodge known as Aynalikavak Kasri. This is an original 18 century building which is now open to the public.

Faience revetment from the facade of the Eyüp Sultan mosque

The Bosphorus and the Rumeli Hisar Fortress

THE GALATA BRIDGE

This bridge links old Istanbul with Galata and Beyoğlu, over the Golden Horn. A bridge was planned during the reign of Bayezit II (148!-1512), for which Michelangelo was contacted, but no project resulted.

In 1845, a wooden bridge was built here by the mother of Abdülmecit I, and this was later replaced with a metal one.

The present bridge was built by a German firm between 1910 and 1912. It is 468 ms. long and 26 ms. wide. The central section can be opened to allow ships to pass through into the Golden Horn shipyards. (usually at night, between 2 and 4 a.m.). It is situated at a nodal point the area between Eminönü and Karaköy having the densest traffic in the city. Looking over to old Istanbul, towards Eminönü from the bridge, one may see the Yeni mosque, and the monumental mosques dominating the skyline on the hills of the city.

Apart from the Galata bridge, there are two other bridges over the Golden Horn, the Atatürk Bridge and the Haliç Bridge. At the top of the street leading from the Galata bridge to the Atatürk bridge, in Karaköy, is the historical underground, which takes one to Beyoğlu. A Sinan mosque, the Sadrazam Sokullu Mehmet Paşa mosque and Mihrimah Sultan fountain stand at the bottom of the same street.

The Galata Bridge (XIX. century)

The new Galata Bridge

THE GALATA TOWER

This is thought to have been built by the emperor Anastasius I (491-518 A.D.), although there is probably stronger evidence to suggest that it may have been the work of the Genoese to defend them against repeated Byzantine attacks. The Byzantine side of the city was over the Golden Horn in old Istanbul, between the Horn and the Marmara Sea. The Genoese and other foreign powers had their colonies on the other side of the Horn. The sea powers used Galata as a port which was a forward stage in mercantile relations with Byzantium. They must have built the tower for defence purposes. With the same purpose in mind, work was begun on the Galata walls in 1341, and the tower was built in a bend in the walls. We may still see part of the basal walls and moat.

Mehmet II took the tower from the Genoese, and reduced its height to 6.8 ms. (10 arşin). The tower was used as a weather observatory during the reign of Murat III (1514-1595). A large stone staircase leads up to the top gallery. In recent years a lift has been added, while restaurants and night clubs have been built on the other floors.

Galata Tower

Dancer

NUSRETİYE MOSQUE

Situated among ancient military barracks at Tophane, the mosque was built between 1822 and 1826 by Mahmut II (1808-1839). The style is an interesting amalgam of Baroque and Empire. It has several annexes, including a clock room and sebil fountain. Originally surrounded by high walls pierced by court gates, these features of the mosque disappeared when the road was widened during the reign of Abdülaziz I (1861-1876). The clock room and the sebil were moved over from the other side of the road to another site which is where they are today, Hence the true form of the mosque is unknown. It is highly decorated with devices foreign to Turkish art. The inscriptions are the work of the calligrapher Hattat Mustafa Rakim Efendi.

Such works are valuable as an indication of a renaissance, the awakening of a new aesthetic, even of a new world view. The same can be said for the mosques built by Abdülmecit I (1839-1861).

Nusretiye mosque

View of Dolmabahçe Palace from the main facade

Exterior view of the entrance to the gardens of Dolmabahçe Palace

View of Dolmabahçe Palace from the seafront

DOLMABAHÇE PALACE

The district of Dolmabahçe is situated on the European shores of the Bosphorus, at the opening of the straits into the Marmara, between Beşiktaş and Kabataş. It is known to have been infilled from what had been a large bay where the Ottoman fleet amassed for ceremonial departure on naval campaigns. Pavilions and royal lodges were built along the shore from the 15 century onwards, as the sources inform us. In time the bay was silted up and the process of infill began in the reign of Ahmet I (1603-1617). The palace of Dolmabahçe was built on the ground gained by infill, taking its name from the imperial gardens which the sultans chose as the site. Evliya Çelebi, in his "Seyahatname" refers to the gardens as the "Dolmabahçe". During the reign of Ahmet III (1703-1730) the royal estates

were enclosed in a wall containing various imperial lodges. That sultan repaired the walls and the royal buildings. At about that time the royal complex became known as the "Beşiktaş Saray-i Hümayûn".

Sultan Abdülmecit (1839-1861) built the present palace, demolishing some of the earlier buildings to make room for it. This became a grand complex of auxiliary buildings with the main palace in the centre. The building was constructed between 1842-1856. The first section to be completed was the Mabeyn, or administrative quarters which, various inscriptions throughout the palace tell us, was completed in 1847. The latest date is to be found on an inscription over the Valide gate (1855). The palace was completed, according to the daily press, the Ceride-i Havadis dated 11 June, 1856, and Sultan Abdülmecit took up residence there on Friday, 7 June, 1856. Before

View of Dolmabahçe from the gardens

this time, the sultans had always lived in Topkapi Palace.

With the early death of the patron of the palace, Abdülmecit, his successor Abdülaziz (1861-1876) also took up residence here, until his dethronement. His son and successor Murat V lived out his brief reign of three months in the same palace, to be deposed in favour of Abdülhamit.

In his long 33 year reign, the later sultan lived only a few months in Dolmabahçe, later preferring to move to Yıldız Palace which he felt to be safer. On the accession of Mehmet V (Reşad) in 1909, the palace underwent extensive restoration and renovation, and became the imperial seat once more. On his death, the throne went to Vahdettin, who remained in Dolmabahçe for a short time before moving to Yıldız Palace. After his two year reign, in 1922, the sultanate was abolished, and Abdülmecit remained as caliph,

being installed in Dolmabahçe palace. In 1922 the caliphate was abolished and the imperial palaces became the property of the nation.

A number of local and European artists and craftsmen were involved in the building of the palace. The architect and his assistant were Garabet Balyan and Nikogos Balyan. The latter architect, European trained, was responsible for the construction of the Grand Muayede hall, and the Treasury and Imperial gates.

The building has three sections, the administrative Mabeyn, the ceremonial Muayede hall and the Harem. The grand hall, which is in the centre of the building, has the impressive height of 36 ms. It is flanked by the Mabeyn to the south and the Harem to the north. The total area covered by the palace is 14,595 m², and it contains a total of 285 rooms, 43 halls, 6 baths and 6 terraces. The plan follows the basic principles of that of the Turkish

Dome of the Grand Hall

vernacular dwelling adapted to a European stylistic attitude.

The overal style is eclectic, with elements from the Baroque, Rococo and Empire repertoire used side-by-side.

The furnishing of the palace was carried out by Séchan, decorator of the Paris Opera. His furnishings for the palace are in keeping with the magnificence of the building. The furniture, generally of European origin in various styles, included much that was ordered from European workshops for the palace, while some pieces were presented by European and far Eastern countries. Hence it is possible to see a number of different styles of furniture in one room. The furnishing materials are Turkish throughout. Curtains, upholstery and rugs being especially woven, mainly in the imperial factory at Hereke. Other notable decorative features are intricate parquet flooring, crystal chandeliers, candelabra, mirrors, mantelpieces and balustrades.

Among the artefacts decorating the rooms are some notable porcelain ware, mainly vases of European, Far Eastern and Turkish (Yıldız Porcelain Factory) ware. Clocks were also a major decorative feature of the palace which also contains a remarkable collection of paintings, approximately 600 in all. Among them, the names of 120 artists are readable. 19 of them are the works of Zonaro, once court artist, and there are 28 Ayvasovskys, the work of the court painter to Sultan Abdülaziz.

The palace has witnessed some key events in Turkey's recent political history. Here the first parliament convened in the grand hall, in 1877. In 1932 the first Turkish Historical Congress was held here under the directive of Atatürk, and it was here that on 10 November, 1938 that Ataturk died (in room no 71). Today it is a historical building maintained by the National Trust under the auspices of the Turkish Grand National Assembly (TBMM), together with the other imperial palaces.

The Blue Room

The Room of the Stair

DOLMABAHÇE MOSQUE

This was built for the dowager sultan Bezmi Alem Valide Sultan, the mother of Abdülmecid. Rectangular in plan, it is surmounted by a single dome. The striking and elaborate decorations were inspired by the French Empire style. The minarets are constructed in the same spirit, to resemble corinthian columns. The outer court and auxiliary buildings were later removed, leaving the mosque devoid of the decoration afforded by the windowed court wall and court portals, and of its annexes, including a guard station and clock house.

Buildings of this era were generally structurally lacking, due to the use of poor materials. Apparently an attempt was made to compensate for this by elaborate decoration, painted and gilded surfaces.

THE CLOCK TOWER

The clock tower, which stands before the palace gate, was built during the reign of Abdülhamit II. ALthough the architect is not certain, it is thought to have been the work of one of the Balyans. The tower stands 30-40 ms. high, and is of cut stone. It has four floors which narrow gradually towards the top of the tower. It is one of the finer examples of 19 century eclectic architectural decoration to be seen in the city.

Clock towers such as this were erected in a number of Turkish towns and cities during that period, mainly to inform the public of the times for prayer. In addition a barometer, thermometer and such devices as weather vanes giving meteorological information were attached to such towers. Although a later addition, the tower adds a finishing touch to the palace.

Dolmabahçe Palace and the clock tower

YILDIZ PALACE

The palace of Yildiz is set in a pleasant grove overlooking the Bosphorus. It was named after the Yıldız Köşk of Mahmut II (1808-1839). A number of lodges and pavilions were built in the groves in the 19 century, creating an extensive imperial complex. This is the fourth imperial seat, after the Old Palace, Topkapı and Dolmabahçe. Abdülhamit (1876-1909) chose this as his official residence, and added the Şale pavilion, the Malta pavilion and Çadir pavilion. The complex also includes an important library, porcelain factory and such additional buildings as a furniture workshop.

The palace was used during the early republic for various purposes, falling gradually to ruin. In recent years the palace buildings have been restored and put to contemporary use, such as an exhibition hall, museum and café. One of the most interesting buildings in the complex is the Şale Pavilion. The architect is D'Aronco. The pavilion is also known as the Ceremonial Pavilion. Basically two buildings, they were both built for the visits in 1889 and 1898 of Kaiser Wilhem II. Şale Köşk is now used for state protocol. It is a half-timber building three storeys high, and is named phonetically after the chalets of Switzerland and France, which it resembles in outward appearance.

Yıldız Palace

Delicately curved timber staircases link the lower and upper storeys, on which there are approximately fifty rooms. The decoration is a mixture of Baroque, Rococco and Islamic styles, as are the furnishings. The ceremonial hall-Merasim Salonu is covered by a Hereke rug 400 m² in size. Large mirrors are hung on the walls and the ceilings are embellished with gilded panels. Other notable rooms are the Sedefli Oda, which has fine mother-of-pearl inlayed doors, and the Sarı Oda - Yellow room, which is well-known for the scenic paintings on its ceiling. These rooms reflect the 'fin de siecle' taste of the last Ottoman sultans.

During the Republic, the Şale Pavilion was used for a time as a luxury casino, later being used for state receptions. The Shah of Iran, Riza Pehlevi, King Hüseyin of Jordan, Sukharno, President of Indonesia, Haile Selasi of Ethiopia and Charles de Gaulle, President of France, were among the notable guests received here. Since 1985 the pavilion has been open to the public as an historical building.

The Bosphorus Bridge by night

THE BOSPHORUS

The straits of the Bosphorus run between Europe and Asia. They are 32 kms. long and at their narrowest (between the two castles on opposite shores) they are 660 ms. wide. The widest point is at Büyükdere (3.3 kms.). The depth varies from 50 ms. to 120 ms. and there is a surface current from north to south which flows at a speed of 5-4 kms.

There are two main methods of access to the Bosphorus, either by road or by sea. Touristic ferryboats ply the Bosphorus regularly from the Galata bridge to the end of the straits, calling in at ferry stations on both the European and Asian sides on their way. It is an excellent way to see the old wooden yal-dwellings, pavilions and palaces along the shores. Notable among the monuments to be seen are the Dolmabahçe Palace, Çirağan palace and Beylerbeyi palace, as well as the castles of Rumeli Hisar and Anadolu Hisar. Other places of interest include the typical ferryboat stations, architecturally distinctive, and charming fish restaurants. Two suspension bridges link both shores by road. The first was built in 1973, the second in 1988.

The Bosphorus Bridge and Ortakoy Mosque by night

The Bridge of Fatih Sultan Mehmet

The Bosphorus and Rumelihisari

RUMELİHİSARI

This castle was built by Mehmet II to prevent the Byzantine fleet, which had control of the Bosphorus, from communicating with its northern allies. The castle has been variously named throughout history as the Boğazkesen, Nikhisar and Yenihisar. It was built with stone quarried from various places in Anatolia and timber from Izmit and Karadeniz Ereğlisi. 1000 master craftsmen, working with 2000 workers completed the castle in the short time of four months. The Ottoman military and administration at all levels even the sultan worked non-stop, to finish the castle. The construction of each tower was given to a different general, the large tower on the shore being completed by Halil Paşa, the northern tower by Saruca Paşa and the southern tower by Zaganos Paşa. The sultan oversaw the building of the walls between. In 1542 the castle was completed, together with its mosque, fountain, cistern, cellars, stores and armoury, and wooden barracks for the soldiers in the garrison. 400 soldiers were installed in the garrison and a hundred or so cannon were erected on the Hisar Peç tower on the shore. Between these and the cannon of Anadolu Hisari on the opposite shore, control of the Bosphorus was in Ottoman hands. After the conquest both castles gradually lost their strategic importance. Rumelihisari housed a state prison after the 16 century, in the "Karakule" of Saruca Paşa, the northern tower. A number of foreign political prisoners were held in this tower.

The castle is set on a slope which steepens to the west, and stands astride two small hills separated by a flood bed.

Rumelihisari

The three large towers are set in a triangle and separated by 14 small towers, joined by battlements 3-5 ms. long. The castle covers a total area of 30,000 m², and has five portals.

Restored various times over the years, Rumelihisari was left to fall to ruin after the reign of Mahmut II (1808-1839), and the timber structure gradually rotted away. The conical roofs covering the towers were demolished at the begining of the 19 century. The castle was thoroughly restored in 1953 in honour of the 500 th anniversary of the conquest of Istanbul, and converted into an open-air museum.

ANADOLUHİSARI

This was built by Bayezit I (1389-1402), long before the conquest of Istanbul, at the end of the 14 century as the first step in bridging the gap to the Byzantine lines, and to gain control of the Bosphorus. It has been variously called "Yenice hisar", "Akça hisar" or "Güzelce hisar". There is one main tower, with an inner tower and surrounding battlement walls. In the 17 century a small mescit - chapel mosque - and open prayer place - namazgah were added. Mehmet II built Rumelihisari on the opposite shore in order to gain

Anadolu Hisari

complete control of the Bosphorus. With the two castles complete, communication along the Bosphorus was brought to a standstill, leaving the Byzantine capital completely cut off to the north. Both castles were used as prisons after the conquest until well into the 19 century. It was here that erring Janissaries, or foreign envoys or statesmen of Ottoman antagonist states were detained.

KÜÇÜKSU KASRI

During the Ottoman period, summer palaces were built at the various resorts in Istanbul for imperial use, many of which have failed to survive. We know of those that have been destroyed through the sources, particularly engravings. During the reigns of Abdülmecid and Abdülaziz in the 19 century, many timber palaces were demolished and stone buildings in European styles set up in their place. One of the palaces to have lived through that evolution is the Küçüksu Kasrı, which is on the coast road from Üsküdar to Beykoz. We know from the sources that imperial estates existed on the shore at that point after the 17 century, on the site of the present Küçüksu meadows.

The are referred to as the "Bahçe-i Göksu". The region is first thought to have come to the attention of Murat IV (1623-1640). The first buildings to be erected date from the 18 century. Sultan Mahmut I (1730-1754) built a timber palace on the shore, which was restored in later eras and used by different sultans. During the reign of Abdülmecid (1839-1861) the wooden building was pulled down to make way for the present royal lodge. Küçüksu Kasri was com-

The Küçüksu Pavilion

pleted in 1857 by Nikagos Balyan. It contains 10 rooms on three floors. The lower floor houses service areas, such as cellars, kitchens and servants' quarters, while both of the other storeys have a central hall with four flanking roomk. It was built for the brief visits of the sultan, not for permanent habitation. Such palaces were really hunting lodges "Biniş Kasrı". It was restored during the reign of Abdülaziz and later several times. The facade is decorated in Occidental style, and the lodge contains a number of valuable artefacts and works of art. The ceilings are decorated with stucco moulding and tracery, and among the notable features of the interior are polychrome marble mantelpieces, fine parquet and furniture in various European styles. The furnishings and upholstery are Hereke, as are the rugs. Abdülaziz is known to have entertained Prince Edward, Prince of Wales (Edward VII) to lunch here. The building was used for state protocol after the foundation of the Republic. It is now open to the public as an historical building. Beside the lodge stands a marble fountain which was built by Mihrişah Valide Sultan, mother of Selim III, and is a fine example of Baroque. A mescit flanked the lodge too but was demolished in 1956.

The Göksu and Küçüksu streams which flow into the Bosphorus were two of the most favoured resorts in the Ottoman period.

BEYLERBEYİ PALACE

Beylerbeyi Palace was built by Abdülaziz between 1861-1865. The architect was Sergis Balyan. An earlier timber palace built by Mahmut II had previously occupied the site. The terraced grounds of the present palace, including a large pool and a underground tunnel originally belonged to the earlier building. Built as a summer palace, the exterior of the building is Neoclassical in style. The facade is marble and sandstone, the walls are brick infilled. The palace has two sections, Selamlik and Harem, arranged on two floors. Two splendid marble staircases give access to each section independently. The interior decoration and furnishings bear the features of what we may call typical 19 century Ottoman Court style. The palace contains 6 halls and 24 rooms. The room with a pool on the ground floor and Blue room on the first floor, with their flanking chambers constitute the men's quarters. The Harem hall and rooms are smaller in scale. Since this was a summer palace, there is no central heating system, nor are there any chimneys. Apart from room no. 18, which has a parquet-covered floor, all the rooms are floored with rush matting. Three of the rooms have marquetry panelling (rooms no. 18, 21 and 26). The other rooms and halls are either polychrome painted or stucco plastered. The columns of the Blue Room are stuccoed over timber, the stucco painted to resemble marble in cobalt blue. The ceilings are decorated in most unusual forms. Geometrical patterns are noticable together with coloured floral bouquets in medallions. Amidst these decorative devices are panels containing nautical paintings. The patron of the palace, Abdülaziz, was a patron of the navy. Under his guidance the Ottoman fleet became second only to the British fleet. This accounts for the various paintings of ships on the ceilings. It appears that the sultan, also a keen painter, drew sketches for the ceiling decorations himself. It is known that the painter Chelebowsky was brought to the palace to execute the painted ceilings. Some inscriptions are noticable as decorative elements in some of the rooms and halls. Those in the Blue

Room are in gilded 'talik' over a blue ground. They reaffirm the justice of the sultan, and the importance of justice in the running of the affairs of state. They also include supplications, words of praise and the necessary qualities for a good government. Such inscriptions are also to be found on the ceilings of other rooms, namely nos. 19, 23 and 28, some of which are verses and prayers from the Kor'an. Much of the furniture in the palace is European. Gilded suites of chairs amidst gilded cornices, mirrors and consols are prevelant features. These are French in origin. The curtains and upholstery materials are Hereke silks. Most of the rugs were also from Hereke. Two rooms (nos. 17 and 27) contain European Göblen rugs. Some rooms contain inlayed furniture in Anglo-Arab style.

Polychrome Bohemia crystal chandeliers suspended from the ceiling of many rooms lend the palace an entirely different character. Apart from these, vases of Far Eastern, Chinese and Japanese; and European, Sevres and Saxonian origin, may be seen together with Yildiz ware from the porcelain factory founded in the reign of Abdülhamid. A number of notable artists, both local and foreign, worked in the Yildiz porcelain factory, producing rare vases and utility ware. Many of the clocks in the palace, of various sizes, were French. One of the more noticable time pieces is a table clock in the Blue Room, a boulle silver clock weighing 60 kgs.

There are now three bathrooms in the palace, although when it was built there was only one, which was contained within the imperial suite of sultan Abdülaziz, in room no. 24. The two later additions were from the period of Abdülhamit. During the Republic these were modernised and additional facilities added. A number of important statesmen have visited the palace since it was built. Among the most popular guest was the French empress Eugenie. During a visit

View of the interior of Beylerbeyi Palace

to sultan Abdülaziz in 1869, she stayed in Beylerbeyi palace, in the imperial suite, and was given a Turkish bath by a woman brought in from the Beylerbey baths.

The palace's longest resident was the hapless Abdülhamit II who was brought back from exile in Thessalonica to live here in 1912. The deposed sultan occupied suite nos. 8 and 9, to the left of the entrance to the Harem. The sultan, known to be extremely fussy, had a bathroom added to the suite. He died in 1918 in bedroom no.8. His bedroom suite, a Rococco lacquer suite are still to be seen there. In addition the desk, armchair, library and other effects of the sultan can be seen upstairs in room no. 28. A dining suite with chamois-upholstered chairs in the dining rooms (nos. 12 and 21) were brought to

Beylerbeyi from Yıldız by that sultan. They are Viennese Arabesque in style. The jetty of Beylerbeyi is embellished with two shore pavilions. In the upper terrace gardens are other pavilions, namely the Mermer and Sarı pavilions, built during the reign of Mahmut II and the Ahir Pavilion, which is contemporary with the palace and was built during the reign of Sultan Abdülaziz. These buildings are now open to the public. The terraced grounds originally covered an area of 160, 000 m² and included hunting grounds, a zoo, conservatories and formal gardens of note containing plants and trees from all over the world. The grounds were eventually honed down to allow for the building of roads and such buildings as schools, and today they are only half their original area.

View of the interior of Beylerbeyi Palace

The Beylerbeyi Palace

BEYLERBEYİ MOSQUE

The mosque was founded by Abdülhamit I (1773-1789) as a large imperial mosque. The sultan's only other large scale public building was the complex not far from the Valide mosque in Eminönü. The mosque in Beylerbeyi was completed for the dowager sultan Rabia Sultan in 1778. It was built on the site of the chambers of the sacred relics from the old Beylerbeyi palace.

The mosque is totally under the influence of European decorative styles, although the walls are revetted with faience from an earlier period. The most distinctive feature of mosques of that period was the incorporation of the imperial lodge into the main building, whereas in earlier eras, these had been separate annexes. In Beylerbeyi, the lodge is over the portico of the mosque, making this a two-storey structure. Such lodges were designed as a small audience room and lounge for the sultan on his way to the Friday prayers.

Beylerbeyi mosque

ÜSKÜDAR

This is a district on the Asian shore of the Bosphorus, with narrow streets lined with wooden houses, which has managed to preserve some authentic oriental character. There are a number of hans, baths, medreses, mosques, fountains and türbes lending to this effect. It is a place not to be missed by the visitor to Istanbul, the Marmara and Bosphorus. Here too are the fascinating gravestones of a very old Turkish graveyard', the Karacaahmet Cemetry. Other places of interest in the vicinity include the Selimiye Barracks, dating from the Ottoman period, the period railway station of Haydapaşa and finally Kadiköy (Chalcedon) itself.

The Greeks called Üsküdar Chrysopolis, and it was known as the port of Chalcedon, a very well-known town. Xenephon passed here with an army of 10,000 in the fourth century B.C. and in 324 A.D., Constantine I defeated his rival Licinius here. The district became independent. It was subsequently sacked twice during the Arab and Persian sieges of Istanbul in the 7 and 8 centuries. During the Turkish period it became an important centre of trade. Mosques and caravansarais were built there. It was the end of the Anatolian trade route, and the start of the yearly pilgrimage to Mecca. With the construction of the Baghdad railway, Üsküdar gradually lost its importance.

Travelling to Üsküdar by boat from Eminönü, on arrival at Üsküdar one sees the fountain of Ahmet III on the square behind the quay. Built in 1728, it is, like the fountain before Topkapi Palace which it resembles, Rococco in style, with all the features of the "Tulip period". Immediately behind the fountain stands the Mihrimah Sultan Mosque, otherwise known as the Iskele mosque. It was built by the architect Sinan in 1547, for Mihrimah Sultan, daughter of Süleyman

Üsküdar boat station

I and wife of Rüstem Paşa. South of the square is the Yeni Valide mosque, built for Gülnuş, the mother of Ahmet III. Her round mausoleum flanks the mosque. The stone tomb has no roof, but is covered by an iron, dome-shaped grill. The open roof may have been an expression of the desire of the deceased for the blessings of God to rain upon her soul. In Islam, the rain is regarded as God's mercy.

The mosque was completed in 1710, and the dowager sultan was buried in the tomb in 1716.

Further to the west stands a small mosque on the quayside, the Şemsi Paşa mosque (also known as the Kuşkonmaz mosque) which was built in 1580 by Sinan for the vizier-poet Şemsi Paşa.

RUM MEHMET PAŞA MOSQUE

This stands on a high promontory, and was one of the first mosques built after the conquest of Istanbul. The patron was the vizier Mehmet Paşa (who was of Greek origin). The dome of this brick mosque is supported by four piers.

ÇİNİLİ MOSQUE

Built for Mahpeyker Kösem Sultan, the wife of Ahmet I and the mother of the sultans Ibrahim and Murat IV, this mosque is renowned for its tiles. Tiled revetments cover both the interior and the facade of the mosque. The Eski Valide mosque stands to the south of the Çinili mosque. This was built for Nurbanu Valide Sultan, the wife of Selim II and the mother of Murat III in 1583. The mihrab is decorated with fine faience.

Üsküdar

LEANDER'S TOWER (KIZ KULESİ)

This ancient tower stands on a rocky outcrop at the entrance to the Bosphorus just offshore Üsküdar. It is presently used as a lighthouse.

The original tower was built in the 12 century by the Byzantine emperor, Manuel Comnenos (1143-1180), who aimed to find a firm foundation for the chain which was used to close off the Bosphorus to sea traffic. There are countless legends about the tower. The best-known of which is that of Constantine's daughter, said to be extremely beautiful. According to the legend, a fortuneteller told the emperor that his daughter would be bitten by a snake and die. The emperor built a tower in the sea and shut up his daughter in it to save her. One day a snake, hidden in a basket of grapes which had been sent to the princess, bit her and she died. The prophecy came true. This legend gave the tower its popular name - kiz kulesi - maiden's tower.

The Maiden's Tower

THE PRINCES ISLANDS

The Princes islands stand offshore Istanbul, in the south-east Marmara. Called the princes' islands as they were the favoured resorts of the Byzantine princes, they are 18-28 kms. away from the city. Still Istanbul's resort, they can be reached via boat from Kabataş. There are 5 small and 4 large islands in the group, five of which are inhabited and may be reached by boat. They are covered with the summer houses of the Istanbullus. Only horse-drawn phaetons and donkeys plie the islands' roads. The boat visits the islands in the following order:

Kınalı: 1.3 kms², this is the island closest to Istanbul. It has a distinctive band of reddish cliffs along the shoreline, giving it its Turkish name meaning 'henna'. There is a Byzantine monastery on the island which housed a number of princes and noblemen among the devotees. Some traces of the original walls of the monastery still stand on the hilltops of the island.

Burgaz: This covers an area of 1.5 kms.². The remains of two Byzantine monasteries are known on this island. On the site of the present village church originally stood a building founded by the empress Theodora in 842 A.D. It was here that the patriarch Methodius was imprisoned for seven years.

The highest point on the island is 165 ms. and possesses a fine view.

Heybeli: Covers an area of 2.3 kms.². Once known as Chalkitis, (copper island) as it possessed a copper mine, its present name is derived from its shape (sackshape). The pine-covered island has many hotels and restaurants and is a pleasant place for a holiday. There were monasteries on each of the three hills of the island. That on the northernmost hill,

Kınalı Island

the monastery of the Holy Trinity, was probably founded in 850 A.D. and was rebuilt in 1844 by the Patriarch Germenos IV. Today it is a seminary, possessing an important library and a renowned Iconostasis. On the east of the island, where once stood the ancient Panagia Camariotissa monastery, an orthodox orphanage was later founded. Later the Turkish Naval School was founded there in 1942.

Büyük Ada: Measures 5.4 kms² and is the largest and best known of the islands.

Renowned for its fine climate, pleasant woods and beaches, it possesses a number of resorts. Known in ancient times as Pitiusa, it has two hills, which are covered with gum cistus shrub. The hill to the north, Isatepe is surmounted by the monastery of Christ, built in 1547. At the top of the southern hill, at a height of 203 ms. is the monastery of Haghia Georgos (Aya Yorgi), where the remains of a monastery probably originally dating to the 6 century can still be seen.

Burgaz Island

127

Dilburnu point, Büyükada (Princes' Islands)

Büyükada and Heybeliada (Princes' Islands)

128